For Sissy –
Leader, compañera, and woman of great gifts who doesn't

ABOLISHING THE WAR SYSTEM

give up or let us give up,

Love,

Marc Pilisuk

July, 1996

The Normative International Relations Series
of Aletheia Press

Vietnam and International Law: An Analysis of International Law and the Use of Force, and the Precedent of Vietnam for Subsequent Interventions by The Lawyers Committee on American Policy Toward Vietnam, Richard Falk, Chair; John H.E. Fried, Rapporteur.

In re More Than 50,000 Nuclear Weapons: Analyses of the Illegality of Nuclear Weapons Under International Law by Francis A. Boyle, Alfred P. Rubin, Burns H. Weston, Sean MacBride, Richard Falk, Dorothy Hodgkin, Maurice Wilkins, and Peter Weiss, with an introduction by Burns H. Weston.

The World Court Project on Nuclear Weapons and International Law: A Joint Project of the International Association of Lawyers Against Nuclear Arms, the International Peace Bureau, and the International Physicians for the Prevention of Nuclear War; Legal Memorandum by Nicholas Grief, Foreword by Peter Weiss and Saul Mendlovitz.

Abolishing the War System: The Disarmament and International Law Project of the Institute for Policy Studies and the Lawyers Committee on Nuclear Policy; Marcus G. Raskin, Project Director.

ABOLISHING THE WAR SYSTEM

The Disarmament and International Law Project
of the Institute for Policy Studies and the
Lawyers Committee on Nuclear Policy

MARCUS G. RASKIN, PROJECT DIRECTOR

ALETHEIA PRESS
Northampton, Massachusetts

Aletheia Press
P.O. Box 1178
Northampton, Massachusetts 01061

Copyright ©1992 by Aletheia Press
All rights reserved

Chapter Three copyright ©1992 by The Nation
Reprinted with permission

Pablo Picasso, *Guernica* (detail) copyright ©1993
by ARS, N.Y./SPADEM, Paris

Manufactured in the United States of America

Library of Congress Cataloging-in-Publication Data

    Abolishing the war system : the Disarmament and International Law Project of the Institute for Policy Studies and the Lawyers Committee on Nuclear Policy/ Marcus G. Raskin, project director.
        p. cm.
    ISBN 0-9623718-9-0 (lib. bdg) : $30.00.—ISBN 0-9623718-8-2 (pbk) : $12.00
    1. Disarmament I. Raskin, Marcus G.
JX1974.A33   1992
327.1'74—dc20   92-17994
                                                                    CIP

To Cora and Peter Weiss,
who mold dreams and ideals
into practical reality.

The Institute for Policy Studies (IPS), founded in 1963, undertakes critical inquiries on major issues of political and social policy. The public scholars at IPS provide analysis of trends and issues in their historical context in order to seek solutions and understanding of complex political and social problems. IPS Fellows have served as advisers to members of Congress, presidential administrations, movements for democratic social change, churches, and labor organizations. IPS Fellows also appear frequently on public affairs programs, write for major journals, and present social inventions and projects for community-based social change.

The Lawyers Committee on Nuclear Policy (LCNP) mobilizes lawyers and international law on behalf of nuclear disarmament, abolition of all weapons and tactics of mass destruction, and global demilitarization. LCNP is the U.S. affiliate of the International Association of Lawyers Against Nuclear Arms (IALANA) and a U.N. nongovernmental organization. LCNP and IALANA are currently collaborating with other public interest organizations on the World Court Project, an initiative seeking a ruling from the International Court of Justice on the illegality of nuclear weapons policy.

CONTENTS

PREFACE ix
   Marcus Raskin

INTRODUCTION 1
   Abolishing the War System
   Brian D'Agostino

CHAPTER ONE 11
   Disarmament and Common Security:
   Interview
   Marcus Raskin and Howard Friel

CHAPTER TWO 35
   Disarmament and Common Security:
   A Draft Treaty Outline
   Marcus Raskin

CHAPTER THREE 83
   Disarmament and Intelligence
   Marcus Raskin

CHAPTER FOUR 99
   Disarmament and International Law
   Howard Friel

PREFACE

The stunning shift which has occurred in the ideological predisposition of states, and the realization that there are common problems among the peoples of the world which transcend any specific division or conflict, has changed the parameters of the politically possible. The treaty draft on general disarmament and common security presented below is meant to take advantage of this potentially positive but precarious moment in world history by proposing to transform the war system through an international disarmament program that is linked to vibrant international institutions and worldwide citizen participation.

There is a fragile international consciousness now stirring, which seeks a means to shift to a cooperative framework of international relations. The vast majority of the world's nations have assented to this point of view in numerous arms control treaties and resolutions of the United Nations since the partial nuclear test ban treaty (1963), which committed the United States and the former Soviet Union to the principle of general and complete disarmament.

The treaty outlined below is intended to strengthen the determination of the nations, groups, and individuals of the world who are committed to make general disarmament and a common, global security regime a political reality in the twenty-first century.

For their assistance and interest in this project, I wish to thank Louis Sohn, John Mercer, Joan Drake, Seymour Melman, Matt Hooberman, Carl Levan, the Fellows of the Institute for Policy Studies, and members of the Lawyers Committee on Nuclear Policy, especially Peter Weiss, Saul Mendlovitz, Robert Boehm, Burns Weston, Francis Boyle, William Epstein, Anabel Dwyer, and Brian D'Agostino.

I also wish to thank Gar Alperovitz, Richard Barnet, Kai Bird, Greg Bischak, Robert S. Browne, Tony Byrne, Mimi Conway, Christine Files, Barbara D. Finberg, Ellen Frey-Wouters, Ann Fagan Ginger, Edward Gordon, Monica Green, Harry Khalil, David A. Koplow, Olivier Mathey, Ambler H. Moss, Jr., Barbara W. Newell, James Raffel, Henry Richardson, Lester Ruiz,

Michael Shuman, Ingrid Stabb, Judith Stiehm, Edith Tiger, Peter Waack, Michael Wasserman, and Michael G. Wessells.

Very special thanks go to Robert Krinsky and Lynn Raskin. Finally, I would like to thank Howard Friel, the editor of this project, for his perseverance, acuity, and insights throughout, and the Boehm Foundation, the Bydale Foundation, and the John D. and Catherine T. MacArthur Foundation for their support.

Marcus G. Raskin
Washington, D.C.
October 30, 1992

INTRODUCTION

ABOLISHING THE WAR SYSTEM
Brian D'Agostino*

A major issue has developed in the early 1990s that has perhaps signaled an end to the system of world order based on military power. The bad economic news in the United States, and the apparent willingness of the U.S. electorate to turn away an incumbent President closely associated with the national security establishment, indicates that it may no longer be politically feasible for the United States to maintain its enormously expensive global military apparatus at the expense of its domestic economy. Perhaps it is now manifest that a half-century of war mobilization—involving a long-standing, wealth-depleting public subsidy of the Pentagon and its contractors—has ruined the economy of the United States.

While the postwar European and Asian economies invested in civilian production, the United States withdrew investment from these areas, squandering the talent of engineers, scientists, and skilled workers, and wasting capital goods and raw materials on armaments that made no net contribution to our civilian economy. The loss of foreign and domestic markets by U.S. industry, the attendant balance of payments deficit and structural unemployment, the out-of-control national debt, and the deterioration of our civilian infrastructure were all closely related to our multi-trillion dollar diversion of national resources to the managers of military power. A similar, severe economic sacrifice was made in the Soviet Union, resulting in its economic and political collapse in 1991.

While these developments indicate the end of an era, they do not prescribe the kind of world order that will now prevail. Important questions still need to be asked—and answered. Will the United States support genuine global reform

---

*Brian D'Agostino is Executive Director of the Lawyers Committee on Nuclear Policy.

through the United Nations, or will we continue to squander our diplomatic energies trying to block such reform? Will the president and the Congress develop and promote a serious and far-reaching program of economic conversion, or will the threats of defense industry unemployment lock our society into a myopic continuation of military Keynesianism, but on a gradually decreasing scale? These are the questions that will concern us for the remainder of the 1990s. This book is intended to focus the debate squarely on one of those questions: What multilateral disarmament and security arrangements should the United States promote in conjunction with our transition from a war economy to an economy that develops our people, protects our environment, and promotes a just and democratic society?

THE WAR SYSTEM'S CRISIS OF LEGITIMACY

As the world tries to imagine a geopolitical future beyond U.S.-Soviet bipolarism, a structure that collapsed with the Soviet Union, we face fundamental alternatives. While there are undoubtedly a number of such alternatives, the most important three of these can perhaps be formulated as follows.

First, a "concert of great powers" could simply take up where bipolarism left off. This development would maintain the system of armed nation states essentially in its present form, and would most likely involve broader geopolitical authority for Japan and Germany, perhaps giving these two nations approximate world-management parity with the United States. The realization of this alternative would further dissipate already strained economic resources within the industrialized nations, would virtually preclude the possibility of retooling our economies with ecologically sustainable technologies, and would most likely precipitate military competition among the chief economic competitors, perhaps prompting war or the threat of war.

A second alternative was presented in the "Five Year Defense Plan (FYDP) of the United States, 1994-1999," which described a global system revolving around the world-order prescriptions and predominant military power of the United States. The realization of this plan—supported in the presidential campaign by President George Bush and, to a slightly lesser extent, by Governor Bill Clinton—would deepen an already severe economic crisis in the United States, further deindustrializing the U.S. economy for the foreseeable future.

A third alternative representing a substantial departure from the previous scenarios is also possible: Responsible leaders and citizens in the United States and around the world could seize the opportunity created by the end of the cold war and press for genuine global demilitarization and a new system of cooperative security. Only this alternative, which amounts to abolition of the war system, is compatible with a humane and ecologically sustainable future.

It may seem at first glance that abolishing the war system, however desirable, is not politically feasible. A close examination of international legal norms, and growing international support for the integration of such norms in the structures of international relations, suggests that the demilitarization goal is more feasible than one might think. In fact, as these norms grow stronger, the violence-oriented alternatives described above will become less politically feasible, and the demilitarization alternative will become more feasible.

Howard Friel's chapter on "Disarmament and International Law" introduces the rules and principles of international law that work to encourage the abolition of national and global military structures. Friel's analysis revolves around the increasing illegitimacy of two pivots of the war system: nuclear forces and other weapons of mass destruction, and conventional forces and offensive armaments generally.

With regard to the current legal status of weapons of mass destruction, biological weapons have been outlawed since 1972, and negotiations on a convention outlawing chemical weapons were completed in 1992. Later this decade, the International Court of Justice is expected to render an advisory opinion on the legality of the use and threat of use of nuclear weapons. If the Court finds use and threat illegal under international law, the opinion will put pressure on the nuclear powers to move toward nuclear disarmament as required under the 1968 Nuclear Non-Proliferation treaty. Friel shows how these and other developments represent a codification and strengthening of norms against weapons of mass destruction that are rooted in the fundamental principles of customary and conventional international law.

The Raskin disarmament treaty that is published below as the centerpiece of this project makes an important contribution to the abolition of weapons of mass destruction. In order for such abolition to be universal and effective, a global inspection regime proportionate to the task would be necessary. Furthermore, bureaucratic methods of inspection would have to be supplemented with an unprecedented, massive involvement of civilian populations in the task of detecting and reporting clandestine weapons production. The Raskin Treaty breaks new ground on both these requirements for abolishing weapons of mass destruction.

The second international legal norm that works against continuation of the war system is the increasing illegitimacy of aggressive war and the offensive force structures and military doctrines associated with it. This norm is embodied most notably in the United Nations Charter, which prohibits the use and threat of use of force in international relations, with the sole and narrow exception being the force needed to repel an armed invasion of a country's territory. Friel identifies the military doctrine most consistent with this normative principle to be that of "nonoffensive defense" (NOD), variants of which are also known as "defensive defense," "reasonable sufficiency," and "qualitative disarmament."

The NOD doctrine specifies the level and type of forces to which a country could disarm without sacrificing its national security—defined as the capacity to repel armed invasions of its territory. These forces would typically be limited to air defense and border and coast guard forces, equipped with anti-aircraft, anti-armor, and anti-ship weapons. Long-range warplanes, warships, tanks, and offense-capable forces generally would play no role in an NOD force structure, thereby establishing a stable military environment with very low levels of armaments. Disarmament down to nonoffensive defense levels would liberate vast segments of existing military budgets for socially responsible uses.

In a multilateral NOD regime, fewer and fewer forces would be necessary for territorial defense. This arises out of the basic military principle that fewer forces are necessary to successfully defend a territory than to invade it. This means that when country A disarms to the NOD level, it will pose a relatively small threat of invasion to neighboring country B, which will then require even less capability for its territorial defense. Country A will therefore eventually be able to satisfy the NOD criterion with fewer forces than before Country B demilitarized, and so on. Adoption of the NOD norm on a multilateral basis would ultimately lead to an end-stage of disarmament with very low, stable levels of defensive forces.

At first glance, Operation Desert Storm may perhaps be seen as a setback for the normative principle of territorial defense. Here was a case where reversing an armed invasion of a small country by a larger aggressor apparently required an even larger offensive capability, in this case wielded primarily by the United States. It should be noted, however, that this situation arose only because Iraq had maintained a massive offensive capability in violation of the NOD norm. The lesson to be drawn from Desert Storm, therefore, is that countries possessing inadequate capability to invade their neighbors will probably not do so, and that countries possessing the capability to invade their neighbors may, in fact, do so with devastating consequences to human life, to regional environments, and with risk of wider war.

Another lesson to be drawn from Desert Storm is that no single country should retain the military and political power to effectively manipulate the United Nations into endorsing a *de-facto,* unilateral military action under the technical guise of a multilateral, U.N.-sponsored action. Thus, to avoid future mis-use of capabilities earmarked for U.N. collective defense and peacekeeping actions, no state under the Raskin Treaty is permitted to retain military capabilities that would disturb the balance and integrity of the nonoffensive defense regime. Instead, designated capabilities from selected states would be placed under the command of the Military Staff Committee of the United Nations according to the "separation of capabilities" principle. (See Raskin Treaty Article 2[6].) The implementation of the "separation of capabilities" in the final stage of the disarmament process would permit designated states, in the aggregate, to retain collective defense and peacekeeping forces available only to the United Nations. However, the partitioning of these U.N.-available forces would be configured in such a way that no individual state or plausible grouping of states would possess a capability to attack or invade any other state. Thus, due to the "separation of capabilities" design for U.N.-available forces, the integrity of the nonoffensive regime is maintained, protection against clandestine treaty breakout is maintained, and aggregate capability is maintained to respond to a possible Iraq-style attack in the future. These U.N.-available forces would belong exclusively to the United Nations, and all salaries, expenses, and equipment would be paid by the United Nations.

A third legal norm examined by Raskin in chapter 3 relates to special warfare forces, including covert operations capabilities—a capability that is often omitted or minimized in arms control and disarmament discussions. The watershed development in this area was the 1986 ruling of the International Court of Justice in *Nicaragua v. United States.* The Court ruled that covert U.S. military attacks in and against Nicaragua, including U.S.-supplied *contra* attacks, violated Nicaragua's territorial sovereignty in violation of international law.

While the United States first sought to prevent this ruling, and then ignored it once it was rendered, this stance isolated U.S. leaders in world opinion and has revealed the extent to which a global consensus has developed in support of the international legal norms that prohibit the aggressive use of force—the same legal norms that would serve as the basis for a defense-oriented, disarmament regime.

In summary, the eroding legitimacy of nuclear weapons, wars of aggression (and the offensive weaponry associated with them), and covert operations suggests that either of the "great powers" approaches to world order, far from being the political course of least resistance, are likely to become increasingly untenable. The question now should be not whether it is politically feasible to abolish the war system, but which policy framework will be most serviceable for doing so.

Time for an Old Blueprint

Efforts to achieve general disarmament need not and ought not start from scratch. As described in Howard Friel's interview with Marcus Raskin, a former Kennedy administration official, former Soviet and U.S. leaders Nikita

Khrushchev and John F. Kennedy presented outline plans on general disarmament to the United Nations in 1962. While these plans never materialized, they nevertheless had a significant impact on world security, helping to shape the 1963 Limited Test Ban Treaty and the 1968 Nuclear Non-Proliferation Treaty. These as well as other arms control treaties state as their ultimate purpose "general and complete disarmament." Raskin's detailed draft treaty is based in part upon the 1962 outline plan.

The Raskin Treaty can serve as a resource and policy vehicle for those seeking to seize the present opportunity for a peaceful and just world order. While the success of this initiative will depend in part on the support of enlightened public officials, political leadership will also need to come from the grass roots, including churches, labor unions, citizen organizations, and individuals who do not have a positive stake in the war system, unlike most government officials and arms control professionals. Dr. Bernard Lown, head of International Physicians for the Prevention of Nuclear War, aptly described the current situation when he remarked that depending on arms control professionals to undertake real disarmament is like looking to boxing referees to outlaw boxing. Since the policy initiatives for disarmament will have to come from the people, this means that the people will need to learn more about the technical problems regarding disarmament and common security.

The general disarmament regime proposed by Raskin would establish an International Disarmament Organization (IDO) under the United Nations that would have responsibility for verifying and facilitating compliance with the treaty. Troops would be decommissioned and military equipment destroyed or converted to peaceful uses in three stages of four years each. Thirty percent of personnel and equipment would be disarmed in stage one, forty percent in stage two, and thirty percent in stage three. For purposes of counting, categories of weaponry are specified by the treaty. International arms transfers would be halted one year after the treaty enters into force.

Each state party to the treaty could choose to initially open its entire territory to inspection or divide its territory into three zones that would become subject to inspection in each stage. Each party could also choose whether to have the inspection performed by the IDO or by the state or states commonly thought to be its military adversaries. Suspected violations of the treaty would be investigated by the IDO, and, if necessary, by the International Court of Justice through a committee of experts appointed for this purpose. The parties would also agree to sanctions for violations of the treaty. The sanctions for specific violations would be determined by the Court and applied by the IDO, or, if necessary, by the U.N. Security Council.

Up to one hundred IDO inspectors would have continuous and unrestricted access to all plants and facilities in each country, including the seat of government. The IDO would also monitor economic conversion plans generated in each country on an annual basis. Because of the limitations of these bureaucratic mechanisms, the treaty also provides for massive citizen involvement in the verification and implementation of general disarmament. Scientific institutes, labor unions, universities, churches, and citizen organizations would all play roles in ensuring their own government's compliance with the general disarmament regime. Reliable and anonymous channels of communication would enable such organizations as well as individual citizens to report suspected violations of the treaty directly to the IDO. The treaty also requires that the Asian and Nuremberg Tribunal standards be incorporated in domestic law and military regulations, which would criminalize all aspects of manufacture of weapons prohibited by the treaty.

The International Court of Justice would have an expanded role in post-disarmament conflict resolution, as would individual citizens and citizen organizations. Signatories of the general disarmament treaty would initially have to include all militarily significant states, but the provisions of the treaty would eventually apply to all states.

Transition to a Peace Economy

Without economic conversion planning, the kind of massive and rapid dismantling of the war system that would occur under the treaty would cause catastrophic economic dislocation. Although the treaty provides for some reporting of economic conversion plans to the IDO, the main responsibility for such planning is left to the national and local levels. An example of how such planning might work can be given for the United States. In place of the weapons production that would otherwise be funded, the federal government could award contracts to prime contractors for a combination of economic conversion planning, job retraining, and public works projects. These contracts would last for two years and would cover the costs of transition to civilian production including salaries of all former defense workers at a rate of ninety percent of their former salaries up to a specified maximum. The ninety percent provision would help bring the former defense salaries into line with civilian pay scales. The maximum-pay provision would avoid extravagant executive salaries. This policy would minimize economic dislocation at the level of individual workers and their families. It would simultaneously benefit the U.S. economy as a whole, which would be plunged further into depression if the purchasing power generated by defense contracts was suddenly terminated.

Beyond the two year transition period, the federal government would continue to take responsibility for long-term job creation by administering public works projects on a permanent basis. The responsibility for converting facilities and personnel to civilian use, however, should be placed at the level of the former bases and factories themselves and surrounding communities—only at that level can information be gathered about the kinds of skills and equipment available at each work site, and how such resources can be utilized to meet civilian needs. Alternative use committees consisting of managers, workers, and community representatives should be established to plan civilian production that can make good use of the available skills, equipment, and facilities.

The shift of revenues from war preparations to the rebuilding of roads, rails, factories, and other capital infrastructure in the wake of cold war neglect will create new demand for civilian production. Civilian enterprises that prove to be economically nonviable should not receive continued public subsidy. It is therefore essential that public subsidies terminate at the end of the two year planning and retraining period. Unemployment created in the wake of failed civilian enterprises can then be handled to whatever extent necessary through federally administered public works projects.

The general disarmament and economic conversion policies outlined above provide specific and practical planning criteria for realizing the alternative of a cooperative and peaceful security regime. But such planning, for both disarmament and conversion, needs to begin as soon as possible. Given existing levels of military overkill, the United States could immediately and unilaterally implement a two year moratorium on all weapons production, testing, research and development without jeopardizing military capabilities for legitimate self-defense. The above conversion idea shows how this could be done with a minimum of economic dislocation. During this two year period, the United States could undertake diplomatic initiatives to all militarily significant states on behalf of a general disarmament plan such as Raskin has developed.

The failure of the United States and the former Soviet Union and other industrialized powers to enact serious and far-reaching economic conversion planning is already having catastrophic consequences, helping to intensify an already obscene international commercial traffic in armaments. Pressed for hard currency, Boris Yeltsin's Russian government resorted recently to arming China with advanced weaponry, while the Bush administration recently sought to maintain defense industry employment by selling advanced fighters to Taiwan and Saudi Arabia. Other examples are numerous. Such short term palliatives merely perpetuate and internationalize the economic pathologies that have ruined powerful economies in the Soviet Union and the United States in the first place.

The Raskin Treaty provides a coherent and practical alternative to continued global militarism and the poverty and ecological degradation associated with it. The extent to which responsible citizens and citizen organizations master such policy ideas is the extent to which we will be able to hold our president and Congress accountable for their inaction. While abolition of the war system may be an idea whose time has come, realization of this idea depends upon the actions of many individual leaders, citizens, and organizations. This book is intended to provide people with the legal and policy expertise needed to make it happen.

CHAPTER ONE

DISARMAMENT AND COMMON SECURITY
Interview with Marcus Raskin

This interview was conducted in Washington, D.C. at the Institute for Policy Studies on March 20-21, 1992, with Marcus G. Raskin, Co-Founder of IPS, and Howard Friel, Publisher and Editor of Aletheia Press.

H.F.: For the purposes of introduction, how would you describe the treaty on general disarmament and common security, which you have authored, and which I will refer to as the "Raskin Treaty"?

M.R.: You are generous to call it the Raskin Treaty. But as you know, treaties such as this grow out of the work of many people. In this case the treaty on general disarmament and common security can be traced back to the 1960s, to the disarmament treaty outline that was developed in the administration of President John Kennedy. And while this treaty is in many ways substantially different from that treaty, nevertheless, its roots are there just the same. The modern concept for such a treaty goes back even further to the statements made at the League of Nations by Maxim Litvinov, as well as to the work of John Dewey and Salmon Levinson, a distinguished corporate lawyer who worked with both Dewey and the U.S. Senate on the concept of the outlawry of war.

Getting back to your question, the treaty is primarily an attempt to organize a body of rational and prudent principles, including fundamental international law principles, and then apply them to the disarmament question. The treaty takes into account the often irrational aspects of global society, but the treaty regime is not overwhelmed by the "irrationalism" of the international system that has often served as a justification for the necessity of war. Thus, the treaty is an orderly and prudent way of beginning to establish a world order that rejects the assumption that every element of international politics is to be governed by war, violence, and repression. The fact that the twentieth century has committed itself to war and violence, and the fact that we are all witness to the product of that commitment, should motivate all of us to look for alternative ways of structuring relationships between nations and groups without resorting to the repression and political silence of authoritarianism.

The treaty itself, I hope, is a carefully constructed disarmament regime that can be used by governments, nongovernmental organizations and groups, and individuals to move us away from a stagnant, casuistic approach to arms control that characterized the several decades of the cold war.

The disarmament process outlined in the treaty is designed to be completed over a twelve-year period. Coinciding with this disarmament period, and, in a sense, illuminated by this process, would be the need for significant institutional change in the United States that would make it possible to complete the disarmament process, and also to deal with a number of problems that we must begin dealing with in any event in order to stop the societal decay in the United States which has become all too obvious in recent years. Many of us do not think it is possible to address these other societal issues too effectively until we have stopped the diversion of our country's resources to the military. But we can discuss this further as the interview progresses if you wish.

H.F.: How did you become involved, in the context of your professional background, with international law and disarmament issues?

M.R.: My interest in international law began at the University of Chicago in the 1950s where I met Quincy Wright, who at the time was the most distinguished international lawyer of his generation, adviser at Nuremberg, and someone who had spent a great deal of time thinking about the United Nations and the U.N. Charter. I was privileged to work with him as a reader in international law, that is, I was his assistant. I became very interested in the use of international law as a means of controlling and transforming military disputes among nations so that a wholly different kind of security system could get started. This was a position held by Quincy Wright. He, among others, including John Dewey, believed that the war system reflected the dark side of civilization and its most sordid aspects, while the principles and rules expressed in international humanitarian law represented the highest ideals and most ennobling aspects. If you take a look at most documents having to do with the philosophic view of public policy from Plato onward, there is quite a literature on the ennobling of war and the use of war as a means of projecting manly characteristics and moral and physical courage. However, the romanticization of the war system is quite contradictory to the principles that a civilized society should value, and to the way a society should function.

This contradiction between war and civilization was pointed out certainly by the end of the nineteenth century by Czar Nicholas of Russia, who called for an international disarmament conference in 1899 due to the economic difficulties that high levels of military spending placed upon his own society even then. It was also pointed out at the end of both the First and Second World Wars. During these two periods, at least a rhetorical, philosophic pretension came to be raised that it was time to go beyond the war system. The problem that we have had since then is that we have not been able to establish the conditions that would enable us to realize the kind of world envisioned in those legal statements and documents. So I took as one purpose in my own work to see to what extent we could show that there were practical applications to the principles of international law and world peace.

H.F.: In a practical sense, then, what kind of an approach to disarmament and international law did you come away with as a result of your work with Quincy Wright at the University of Chicago?

M.R.: Well, I think there were a couple of things that one came away with. One was the idea that international organizations could take up the slack for what States themselves were incapable of doing. It became very clear even during that period, here we are talking about the mid- to late-1950s, that there were clear limits as to what the nation-state was able to do, not with regard to its war-making capabilities since these capabilities were becoming vast, but with regard to its peace-making capabilities, given the international arena of competing interests. Secondly, the existence and stockpiling of nuclear weapons changed the character of war and the threat of war, in the sense that war now posed the threat of extinction.

Of course, the existence of nuclear weapons, modern military organizations, and the proliferation of military technology changed the character of our society here in the United States. What I am referring to, and what Quincy certainly referred to, is that there is a contradiction between democracy on the one hand and a system of international relations which puts war-making institutions in a privileged position *vis-a-vis* the rest of society. The fact is that, during Quincy's time, the idea of disarmament was linked to the preservation of democracy in the United States. In other words, the advocates of developing a disarmament system were also proposing a means to protect democracy. Disarmament, then, was not only a means for the quantitative reduction and elimination of weapons, it was a way of guarding against the encroachment on our democratic institutions by the national security state.

What is important to note is that even those people who did not have a commitment to democracy, but who instead favored the idea of a republic, men such as Herbert Hoover, were committed to disarmament for reasons having to do with the preservation of capitalism and a market economy. Their fear was that the war system built up the authority of the state and that a command economy engaged in long-term military production would be antithetical to free enterprise and capitalism and our peoples' standard of living. These were the reasons that many conservatives in earlier generations supported the idea of disarmament.

Liberals then developed the notion, liberals such as Quincy Wright, that what you had to do was to declare yourself committed to a system of international law that did the following things: that tamed war if it occurred, developed a sufficiently strong and respected international organization to be able to resolve disputes in order to prevent war, and facilitate movement toward global disarmament. That is what grew out of the liberal position as to how to control and transform the war system.

Now, let me just elaborate further on John Dewey's position since I mentioned him earlier, and since it would help explain the context of the liberal position. John Dewey in the 1920s spoke to the idea of the outlawry of war and wrote voluminously on the question in order that humanity might avoid another world war. As you know, the Kellogg-Briand Pact spoke to the outlawry of war, and the United States ratified that treaty in January of 1929. The value of that treaty was limited because nations reserved for themselves the right to defend their global interests as part of self-defense, thus justifying imperialism, and because there was no collective security arrangement which transcended bilateral treaty arrangements. Nevertheless, that treaty became the basis for the American position at Nuremberg to hold the Nazi leadership responsible for breaking the peace.

The reason I mention this is that throughout the 1920s and 1930s, people took very seriously the debate about international law, about the outlawry of war, about even signing a treaty for outlawry of war, however imperfect. All of that fell to pieces with the onslaught of Hitler and, after that, with the coalescence of international politics into the cold war. Yet, even at the height of Truman's and Eisenhower's cold war, there remained in American social and political thought the notion of a pragmatist realism, which took international law and disarmament seriously, was not formulated along the lines of *realpolitik,* and which was finally destroyed in my view in 1961-62. We can talk about how that happened.

H.F.: You mentioned a moment ago that the political conservatives of earlier generations saw the arms race as a threat to American capitalism. How would you respond to people who would argue that it was the arms race and the tremendous military pressure that the United States placed upon the Soviet Union that actually caused its breakup and the emergence of capitalism there and in Eastern Europe?

M.R.: I think the way one has to respond is to look at the U.S. budget deficit and the national debt at this point—indebtedness that was built up over the Reagan and Bush years due primarily to their enormous military expenditures—and recognize the very serious threat this is to our economy and to our people. The debt that we have incurred during the largest increase in military spending in our country's history, from 1980-1992, has bankrupted our country. We now have a $4 trillion national debt, which makes us the largest debtor nation in the world. Before Reagan and Bush assumed office, we were the largest creditor nation in the world. Due to the very large diversion of scientific, engineering, and high technology talent to the military sector over this period, the products of our industrial economy are not competitive in the world market. Thus, we now have the largest trade deficit of any nation in the world. We right now have more people who are unemployed, underemployed, and employed but living below the poverty level than we have ever had at any time in our country's history. There are about ten million children in this country who do not get enough food to eat each day. We have millions of homeless people. And so on. Therefore, I would respond to those people who think that the U.S. economy has benefited from a $3 trillion expenditure on our military and intelligence agencies over the past ten years by saying that they are practicing a very serious game of either self-delusion or political deception.

H.F.: How was it that you went from the University of Chicago in the late 1950s to the Kennedy White House in the early 1960s?

M.R.: In 1957 I graduated from law school and went to Europe for a year to study piano. I returned in 1958 and moved to Washington where I began work as a legislative assistant for a group of congresspeople, and began work, among other things, with issues having to do with "The Liberal Project." This was a group of Congresspeople who had as their purpose the development of an alternative foreign policy beyond the cold war of that period. I later became staff editor to a book called *The Liberal Papers* which caused a great stir when it was published in 1962.

In the congressional elections of 1958, a substantial number of Democrats was elected to Congress who were liberal and who were eager to move in a direction outside of the parameters of cold war ideology, who were committed to international cooperation, and who were also committed to what at the time was a very hot issue—the recognition of China. And so I worked with this group of people. Then, as luck would have it, nearly half of the congressional members for whom I worked lost their seats in the 1960 elections, whereupon I had no place to go but to the National Security Council in President Kennedy's White House. I was hired at that time as a member of the special staff at the National Security Council to McGeorge Bundy, where my responsibility was to work on questions dealing with national security and disarmament.

H.F.: Was the Kennedy White House a good environment for working on disarmament issues?

M.R.: I think the fact is that the Kennedy White House was pretty much of a mixed bag on those issues. On the one hand, President Kennedy had arrived at the White House talking about the missile gap and the need to develop flexible response as a military strategy. As a result the defense budget in the

Kennedy administration went from $39 billion to $51 billion, which by the way caused President Eisenhower to criticize severely this increase in military spending.

By the same token, the Kennedy administration, and especially President Kennedy, had argued that, since fewer than a hundred people worked on disarmament issues under Eisenhower while tens of thousands were working on war plans, more people needed to work on disarmament. So there was this contradictory position in the Kennedy administration between the increase in armaments and the idea that we should be moving toward disarmament.

During the Kennedy and Eisenhower presidencies, there was congressional and public pressure to establish an advocacy agency within the government for arms control and disarmament. While working in Congress, I was privileged to be involved in that effort, and I drafted one of the three bills that was drafted at that time: this was the "Peace Agency" bill. The other two bills advocated the establishment of a Disarmament Agency and an Arms Control Institute.

These different proposals reflected different liberal positions of the period. The proposal for an Arms Control Institute was basically drafted out of the Harvard-M.I.T. arms control seminar that had just taken place. The Disarmament Agency proposal was drafted by Senator Hubert Humphrey, while the Peace Agency proposal—the one that I had worked on—was the Kastenmeier bill. What ultimately happened was that all of these proposals were melded together and an Arms Control and Disarmament Agency was established.

My concern at the time was that the new Arms Control and Disarmament Agency would come to rationalize Defense Department decisions rather than work to present an alternative to the Defense Department's positions. The arms control idea, which really got its start in 1959-60 from the Harvard-M.I.T. group, stood for two things: rationalizing and managing the arms race, and giving intellectuals from the universities a way to talk about national security matters within the framework of fundamental military assumptions, that is to say, without scaring the Pentagon. In a sociological sense these intellectuals—the military and national security intellectuals—were put in a position where they would appear to be taken seriously by the government and where they could act as consultants to the government and so forth. What happened, then, over the course of a few years, was that the idea of disarmament was dropped. By the time President Kennedy was killed, and only a short time after the Arms Control and Disarmament Agency was established, the whole notion of disarmament as an alternative strategy for national security planning had been abandoned.

On the other hand, during this period, there was an attempt on Kennedy's part to press for a general and complete disarmament strategy, and this strategy manifested itself in many forms, for example, in his "Sword of Damocles" speech. Kennedy's interest in disarmament conflicted with the advice of most of his political advisers and arms control experts, including McGeorge Bundy, who believed in arms control, not disarmament. Indeed, if you take a look at Bundy's book, *Danger and Survival,* which deals with the history of nuclear choices over this whole generation, there is virtually no mention of disarmament and no mention of the idea of general and complete disarmament. So McGeorge Bundy's spin on things, and the view of a number of those people at that time, was that disarmament was not a viable option, given their habit of mind.

John McCloy, on the other hand, who during that period was thought to be the chairman of the establishment, pressed for a general and complete disarmament program, and for a time he was President Kennedy's leading advisor on disarmament. Part of his effort, in my view, related to the fact that he was very friendly with Grenville Clark and also with Louis Sohn, who had written an important work on security and disarmament.

The rest of the world saw arms control in negative terms during that period. For example, Alva Myrdal described the arms control process in her book, *The Game of Disarmament,* as a mask for continuing the arms race. She was correct in her assessment. The arms control structure was a management system for the more efficient continuation of the war system.

H.F.: The Arms Control and Disarmament Agency, which, as you just mentioned was established by President Kennedy, produced a prototype treaty outline on general disarmament, is that right?

M.R.: Yes, that's right. It should be noted that work on such a treaty outline began under President Eisenhower with Robert Matteson, who had been an adviser to Harold Stassen when Stassen was Eisenhower's disarmament negotiator.

H.F.: What was your involvement in the development of that treaty outline?

M.R.: Before I answer that question directly, let me take you back for a moment to give you some context to the development of that treaty outline.

When Nikita Khrushchev came to the United States in 1959, he proposed that a general and complete disarmament treaty be completed and implemented within four years. This proposal came at the end of a series of discussions and near agreements between the United States and the Soviet Union on the question of disengagement of both short-range missiles and nuclear weapons from Europe. And deals were almost cut in 1955 and in 1957 for these purposes. The person who spearheaded these negotiations in the United States, aside from Eisenhower himself, was Harold Stassen. Eisenhower's Secretary of State, however, John Foster Dulles, was not a supporter of disarmament or disengagement from Europe. He was more interested in building up Germany and

NATO than in any kind of agreement with the Soviets that would result in independence for Germany from either the United States or NATO. Dulles, therefore, supported no disarmament agreement with the Soviets or any agreement that might result in undercutting NATO. As I mentioned, this was not Stassen's position, but Stassen lost out in his battles with Dulles, and with Richard Nixon as well. At the time Nixon, as Eisenhower's Vice-President, was opposed to either disarmament or arms control.

At the end of the Second World War, the central concern of U.S. foreign policy was how to control Germany. The fear was that since Germany had been critical in starting the First and Second World Wars, it could not be easily controlled, that it had to be controlled, and that the best way to control it was to integrate it as much as possible into the NATO system. The Soviet Union was perceived as a threat, but as a secondary threat to the development of a Western alliance, an Atlantic community as it was called, which would embrace Germany even if the ultimate price to be paid was the rearmament of Germany.

So within the context of this policy scenario, in walks Khrushchev in the late 1950s with a disarmament proposal. Many will recall that he had already reduced unilaterally his own conventional forces, relying on his idea of massive thermonuclear retaliation if a war were to occur. His strategic purpose at this time was to get the United States to agree to a disarmament treaty, and to get the United States to withdraw from its system of military bases around the world. The Americans did not take Khrushchev's disarmament proposal seriously, since it would have required us to take seriously the idea of the transformation of our entire alliance system, which was built up by Dulles and rationalized by the cold war. The Acheson-Dulles architecture would have to have been torn down. The diplomatic posturing at the time, however, was that Khrushchev came to the United States and presented a disarmament proposal, which was received seriously throughout the Third World and in the peace movement in the West.

One of the processes involved in any disarmament discussion is the public relations activity that is directed at the third party always sitting at the negotiating table, that is, the citizenry of the negotiating parties, in this case, the people of the United States and the former Soviet Union. What often happened in situations like this was that each party wanted to demonstrate that it really supported disarmament, that it really wanted to change course, but that the other side did not. So what came out of that period in my view was a three-tiered mode of negotiations: one mode involved advocating one position in public, for public-relations purposes, while pursuing another position in the relative seclusion of the formal negotiations; a second mode involved serious negotiations over one or two incremental steps; and a third one involved the sincere motivation of some negotiators to reach an agreement on comprehensive disarmament. The third mode was never really developed or achieved, the first mode functioned as the negotiating strategies of most arms control negotiations, and the second one resulted in the agreements that we have today, which have permitted the United States to modernize its strategic nuclear arsenal and its conventional sea, land, and air forces on a massive scale.

These negotiating modes reflected, by and large, the different philosophies and attitudes among officials within the government. The philosophy that won out in the end was represented by the idea that the Soviet Union would be more likely to collapse before the United States if we just kept modernizing our strategic and conventional forces, thereby piling on armaments and weapons systems that were permitted by the several arms control agreements that imposed only incremental limitations on this process.

In 1960, then, the United States began preparing a disarmament plan because the Soviets said let's begin negotiating. So the United States, in 1960 under President Eisenhower, prepared a treaty outline. But that treaty was vague in terms of its outline and specific purpose. Nevertheless, that was the plan that was rewritten and modified in 1961 by the Kennedy administration. The people who were most involved in rewriting that plan were in the disarmament agency. The advisers at ACDA who were most involved were Betty Goetz Lall and Louis Sohn. On the White House side, Jerome Wiesner, Spurgeon Keeney, and I were also involved. We had designed an ambitious plan for general and complete disarmament which fell on deaf ears at a meeting of the Foster panel, a panel convened to limit strategic missiles to a level of 1,000 at a time when the United States did not yet have 1,000 strategic missiles. William Foster said that Wall Street would be very upset with the White House proposal and everyone laughed knowingly.

The disarmament plan that was adopted by 1962 was a revised version of the Eisenhower plan. This 1962 disarmament plan, and the one that was presented by the Soviets, were close enough to have constituted a basis for serious negotiation. Indeed, Professor Bernard Feld of M.I.T. wrote an important article showing how both documents were quite compatible. So the possibilities for working toward general disarmament were very real at that time.

Two things then happened which undercut the possibility for serious negotiations. One was a decision to move incrementally and to say that nuclear testing is separate from a general disarmament treaty. That meant that we were going back to an incrementalist position, where we take little pieces and attempt to get an agreement on little pieces. I objected to that position, but in any case that was the position that was taken. I objected because it would take as long or longer to get agreement on a small step as it would be to get agreement on a comprehensive one—and there would be much less payoff. The second was that the main event during this period was a military buildup. In addition to the buildup, extensive covert operations were being conducted at the time, and there was talk about going into Vietnam. So the Kennedy administration was following a "simulopt" policy, a simultaneous options policy, whereby several different policies were pursued, supposedly with the same objectives in mind. In reality, however, the objectives were different, given that one of the options predicates a superiority, while the other one predicates cooperation.

After the Cuban missile crisis, however, as far as I can tell, Kennedy moved toward a disarmament position in a serious way. Evidence is now coming to light, dug out by Robert Krinsky, suggesting that Kennedy was very eager to develop a general disarmament program beyond what existed before. His change was related to the frightening situation that came about during the Cuban missile crisis. Secondly, it seemed very reasonable to cut a deal with the Soviets on an environmental arms control agreement, namely, the partial nuclear test ban treaty. Even for this very modest agreement, however, the president paid a very dear price. He had to agree to an increase in the number of nuclear tests by a factor of three over the course of time.

H.F.: What was the connection, if any, between the disarmament plan that was put forward by the Kennedy administration and the McCloy-Zorin Accord?

M.R.: President Kennedy appointed John McCloy to begin discussions with McCloy's Soviet counterpart, Valerian Zorin, who was a Soviet special ambassador, to work out a set of propositions for negotiations on general and complete disarmament. Those discussions went on over the course of several months in the spring of 1961, and were important for two reasons: It showed the seriousness of purpose that President Kennedy placed on the general and complete disarmament proposition, and it gave the disarmament idea a measure of credibility, since McCloy was seen by both the Soviets and the United States as the head of the establishment. McCloy, an important banker, was seen by Kennedy, and later by Khrushchev, as a kind of *consigliere,* since he had the ear of the White House, Wall Street, the oil companies, and the Ford Foundation. At the same time, Khrushchev also trusted Zorin, who was at the time a special ambassador and deputy foreign minister. So the McCloy-Zorin discussions came to be very important in setting the basis for the general disarmament discussions that went forward in 1962 at the eighteen-nation disarmament conference in Geneva. The United States and the Soviet Union served as co-chairs of that conference, where other nations as well presented their views on how to implement a general and complete disarmament plan.

Now the question is, why did all of this fall apart? What happened? President Kennedy was killed in November of 1963, and the position of the United States with regard to general and complete disarmament began to change after that. Disarmament was no longer an important matter, and incremental steps such as a U.S.-Soviet nonaggression pact were rushed out of the White House upon Kennedy's death. The incrementalist arms control positions now emerged full-blown. Furthermore, the United States was committed to a weapons buildup to meet the requirements of a flexible response policy, which overshadowed any possibility for an alternative. Finally, the entire notion of an alternative was ground up in the Vietnam War, and people just stopped paying serious attention to any sort of disarmament discussion.

H.F.: In 1963 we had the Partial Test Ban Treaty, in 1972 the SALT I Treaty, in 1979 the SALT II Treaty, and in 1991 Bush and Gorbachev signed the START Treaty. And there have been a number of other treaties as well. How have these major treaties contributed to, or detracted from, the idea of disarmament?

M.R.: The first thing to notice about those treaties is that they all begin with the notion of committing the parties to general and complete disarmament. Thus, a strict legislative interpretation of these treaties should lead one to conclude that START and a treaty on conventional arms reductions are to be considered as incremental steps toward general and complete disarmament rather than permanent resting places. Unfortunately, such a reading is far from the public consciousness.

So now the question then is do those treaties fit within a future general and complete disarmament position? I think the answer to that is they certainly don't have to contradict one another, unless the incremental approach is used as a substitute for comprehensive disarmament.

But the key point that needs to be made is that, presently, we in the United States have no overall alternative security program or security regime, nor does any other nation for that matter. We continue to arm and we continue to move on arms control incrementally. Even the significant reduction in strategic nuclear weapons that the START regime looks like it may accomplish is a far cry from disarmament, since each side would still retain about 4,000 modernized strategic nuclear warheads. Furthermore, the START regime does not reflect new thinking in terms of alternative security, but merely a reduction of a bloated strategic nuclear weapons inventory, continuing modernization of the air and sea legs of the strategic triad, and an effort to maintain a very powerful strategic nuclear arsenal in the long haul in the context of what will no doubt be a very severe fiscal environment in the coming decades.

So the basic frame of reference that we still have today, even though the cold war is over, is the war system frame of reference. Because the United States has emerged as the single military superpower in the world, the question that we as citizens have to ask is: Is this what the United States should be in the world, or can it operate as a "citizen" within the context of a world cooperation arrangement which moves toward a global agreement on disarmament? I am persuaded that we are now experiencing a turning point in history that could make a world cooperation model possible. Some will argue that we need overwhelming military force because we are becoming economically weak, and that we need our military power to compensate for our economic decline. But this argument is what I would call a neurotic policy, because our military superpower status exacerbates our long term economic decline.

H.F.: Addressing the Raskin Treaty specifically, how does the treaty work toward a world cooperation model?

M.R.: It recognizes the problem of the arms race and the war system as multilayered: economic, military, legal, and political. It recognizes the importance of personal responsibility, international institutions, and transnational relationships among citizens groups, such as among scientists. It represents a clean break from the conflict-, paranoia-dominated form of international relations. It is a statement of saying that we now recognize that there are other problems in the world that are far more significant than the ones that bound us to a twilight struggle during the Second World War and the cold war. And these more important problems have to do with the environment, economic disparity, human rights violations, decaying institutions, and historic ethnic and religious struggles.

Secondly, the treaty recognizes the fact that the war system itself is an incredible burden on humanity, costing the citizens of the world $14 trillion since 1945. The United States has suffered enormously as a result of it, from wasted resources to the constant lying and manipulation of the public. At present in the United States, because there has been no alternative regime—that is to say, no alternative security and disarmament system that was debated in the universities, political parties, labor unions, community organizations and churches—politicians and diplomats, always the last to get the message, have been left at a loss to know what to do after the end of the cold war. There's nothing in place as an alternative. And so the third thing that is now required and addressed in the treaty, at least in a general sense, is that this is an alternative regime for proceeding over the course of this next generation. It does so by a cutback across the board down to as close to one hundred percent as possible of all weapons and armed forces in the world, and it does so in terms of the different levels and categories in which each of the various nations possess armaments. It calls for the establishment of an international system of inquiry and, if you will, control of how this process is to go forward through a Board of Inquirers, through the United Nations, through other mechanisms presented in the document itself. It brings forth the idea of a new kind of international organization and regime.

Linked to that is a new sense of personal responsibility and oversight that will give life to the Nuremberg responsibility of government officials, which is to be internalized in the domestic laws of each signatory to the treaty. The treaty would also give standing to different groups that are not part of the government to police the treaty. These groups would have an opportunity to notify an international Board of Inquiry of possible treaty violations. It also establishes a role for the International Court of Justice in the disarmament and security process by assigning "masters" to study and recommend fines regarding violations.

H.F.: Now when you mention Nuremberg accountability, this brings to mind the work of a number of prominent international lawyers who have assigned Nuremberg accountability to those involved in the manufacture of nuclear weapons and their planned and practiced use. Since your treaty seeks the abolition of all nuclear weapons, is there an international law basis for this goal, and what are your views regarding the alleged illegality and criminality of nuclear weapons?

M.R.: When you get to the question—Are nuclear weapons illegal and criminal?—I think we have to divide the question into two parts relating to the use of nuclear weapons and the threat of use of nuclear weapons.

I don't have any doubt in my mind that the use of nuclear weapons is illegal under international law, violating as it does the customary laws of war, the Nuremberg Principles, and the United Nations Charter. Regarding the threat of use of nuclear weapons and the deterrence doctrine that has developed out of the Second World War, I don't see the legality of this policy either, involving as it does the threat of mass destruction of innocent populations. If you look at this deterrence policy, not as a strategic question, but as a legal and criminal question, it seems to me that from the very beginning the use and threat of use of nuclear weapons should have been declared illegal and forbidden.

Now the question is how to get rid of them if it is the case that they are illegal and criminal. What is the means of getting rid of them when even our most genteel and civilized leaders have used them for deterrence purposes, that is to say, used them to threaten the destruction of innocent populations, and when each of the permanent members of the U.N. Security Council has a nuclear weapons arsenal and plans for its use. Within the treaty document, I have alluded to a variety of ways of how that can be done. You have to begin by making public the numbers of nuclear warheads, delivery vehicles and launchers that you have, you have to have assurance, inspection, and verification, both to verify those numbers and to monitor the disarmament process throughout each of its stages. I suggest the establishment of a registry to be sure that scientists and technologists are not working on any aspect of these weapons, except for their destruction. I have also suggested a full series of other means such as a zonal inspection system aimed at nuclear and conventional comprehensive disarmament to cut back over a period of twelve years.

H.F.: In the second half of the 1980s, former Soviet President Mikhail Gorbachev put forward a number of disarmament initiatives that were very comprehensive and credible and which received considerable support from the international community, yet the United States rejected almost every one of them. What conditions would have to develop in the United States for your disarmament proposal to be accepted here by the political and intellectual establishment, the Pentagon, and the defense corporations?

M.R.: The first point in response is to ask—What is the purpose of armaments? If the purpose of armaments is to threaten others and to use them to support an imperial policy, there is not going to be very much that one is able to say to convince those who have that position. If on the other hand, there is interest in developing a security system which allows the United States to begin its own regeneration, its own rebuilding, and allows for the twenty-first century to be different from the twentieth century in the sense of removing the war system, then it seems to me that we have a very great deal to talk about with each particular group. Let us start with the military.

The interests of the U.S. military prior to World War II were predominantly linked to the protection of the land and institutions of the United States. After World War II, however, the United States saw itself as having what was called global responsibilities, and the military's position changed. It no longer concerned itself primarily with defending the territory of the United States and its institutions, but adopted a policy of "forward defense" around the world, which of course was actually a network of forward-based occupation and interventionary forces. These so-called global responsibilities required the United States to bear a great financial and military burden, and it became a very costly enterprise. For example, even now the United States funds NATO in the amount of about $150 billion a year, for a purpose that is not clear to anyone. There's no real enemy, and we are not even controlling Germany, which was one of our primary purposes before. Indeed, we are now witness to Germany and France developing their own bilateral military arrangement and Germany establishing regional hegemony economically through the deutsche mark.

What citizens must do is to go to the military and say: Are you prepared to participate in the regeneration of American life, are you prepared to do it by helping in the development of a world security plan, and are you prepared now over the course of a twelve-year or so period to transform the military forces of the United States if you understand that other nations were doing the same, and if there was a new kind of world security system that you would help develop? If you ask that question, I think you will get the following response: Show us what this world security is going to be like? And this is where the disarmament and international law project that we have initiated becomes important in terms of trying to figure out how such a security arrangement would be structured, and what the process of disarmament would be simultaneous to the development of this world security system.

Second, people would ask in a vested interest way—We have millions of individuals who are now more or less caught in the national security defense world, what are you going to do for them? My view of what we have to do in the United States is to generate a National Security Adjustment Act, which would work to help subsidize Pentagon and C.I.A. people to get out of the warmaking business, to start their own businesses, to retrain themselves for other careers, or to go back to school, perhaps, for advanced degrees and retraining in other viable fields. Related to these efforts, alternative use committees should be established where corporations are prepared to work with workers to begin the transformation or conversion of their military corporations.

Another aspect of this would be to re-work the G.I. Bill and, again, this would also be part of the National Security Adjustment Act, to the point where those people who are involved with the military over a period of time, over this twelve to fifteen year period, are in fact given sufficient funds to go back to school and given sufficient subsidies to begin new careers. Now we do have a G.I. Bill in place at this point, but it is not adequate. So comprehensive adjustment legislation would have to become a part of the dismantling of the cold war national security state structure.

With regard to the universities and the intellectual community, the problem that we have here is that the universities and knowledge workers have lost their pragmatist bent, pragmatist in the best sense, that they do not see or work for a better future, and they don't see how a better future could be concretized into reality. So people at the universities neither know the past nor are they able to use what it is they know for development of a better future. They're caught in the process of specialization, or worse, they are closely affiliated, either ideologically or financially, with the national security state function. So one of the things that we will need to develop during this next period of time is a continuous dialogue to show that an alternative direction can be developed in the world, and that knowledge workers and universities have an intellectual and citizen responsibility for helping in the development of that direction.

As part of that effort, and knowing that we are at the end of an age, the institutions and people that we were just talking about must understand the need for change and regeneration. They must think of their institutions and social roles in new ways. If it is the case that ethnic and racial tensions still exist, that we have decaying, overpopulated cities, a terrible AIDS epidemic, environmental difficulties of the most mammoth kind, a whole new set of problems and dilemmas resulting from the kinds of knowledge developed over the last couple of generations, and if the traditional ruling class in this country, consisting mostly of white males, is reluctant to recognize the struggle of women and nonwhites for equality, it is obviously past time for the universities to recast the things that they think about and what it is they work on in order to address these issues.

Now if you ask me in an elite organizing way how to move the treaty forward, it seems to me that we can put it on the agenda by organizing a group of a half-dozen senators to press forward with this particular idea, and also to get support from other nations, from other leaders around the world, to support a disarmament and common security program.

H.F.: Speaking a bit more to the relationship between disarmament and the economy, what would need to be changed in the economy of the United States if a treaty on general disarmament was agreed upon by the world community and implemented?

M.R.: We have to remember a couple of things about the U.S. economy and where it came from since 1939. Remember that there was a worldwide depression going into the Second World War with the United States suffering a great deal. And that coming out of World War II the fear of most people was that we would go back into a depression at the end of the war. Indeed, toward the end of the war, President Roosevelt put forward the idea of an Economic Bill of Rights in which the G.I. Bill was one of the basic programs. The Economic Bill of Rights consisted of eight specific rights which many advocated as the new Bill of Rights for the American people. Coming out of the cold war, we don't have any of that at this point, we don't have an economic or social bill of rights that people are prepared to put forward, and there's no strong formation within the United States of a social or political sort to press for those sorts of programs. A citizens movement for economic and social rights, including the rights to peace and individual dignity, would help us to extricate ourselves out of fifty years of war and cold war.

At the end of the Second World War there was a more vibrant labor movement, there was a very clear sense that servicemen—soldiers, sailors, and air force people—had to be compensated for the war, otherwise there would have been a very strong sense in the United States of revolt if the war had not brought about any social or economic change. There is no sense at this point, unfortunately, that a similar approach needs to be developed now. For example, while there is a full employment act on the books, the Humphrey-Hawkins Act, the policies of the Reagan and Bush administrations over their twelve years accepted, if not stimulated, unemployment as a permanent feature of our economy. These people rejected any concept of an Economic Bill of Rights. We still have an unfavorable situation in terms of social and political consciousness in American life and this in my view needs to change.

Now when we come to the question of the corporations, corporations at the end of the Second World War identified far more with the United States than they do today. U.S. corporations, while in the last analysis are U.S. corporations, are in fact global organizations and their identification to the United States is much weaker than it was at the end of the Second World War.

During the cold war, a whole system of arrangements was made for U.S. corporations to go abroad, to, in effect, serve as economic and political outposts for the American national security state. And what has happened, of course, is the globalization of capital and a weakening of responsibility of American capitalism to American society. Now those corporations which were national security corporations, whose sole or primary source of business and revenues was the Pentagon, are now in some trouble because they are being forced to compete for business and contracts and market share with corporations that have not been previously dependent upon the Pentagon. Also, as long as the United States has a deficit, the corporations compete with the United States for capital on the capital markets, so that causes a problem for them. This latter problem, that of the deficit, bears mention. Over the course of the last thirty years, corporate taxes have virtually disappeared as has the progressive tax rate. Furthermore, substantial subsidies were given to American capital to go ahead as outposts of imperial triumphalism. These are central causes of the deficit, aside from the national security budgets of $375 billion a year.

H.F.: Let's continue to focus on disarmament and the economy for a bit more. Does economic conversion, in the context of implementation of a disarmament treaty, refer primarily to retraining people who worked within the military industry, or does it also refer to a reindustrialization policy? If so, what kind of reindustrialization do we need to see?

M.R.: The reindustrialization question, from my perspective, should deal with not just reindustrialization, but rather with the questions: What sort of society do we want to have and on what level of technological sophistication? What new kinds of production and production systems will be required? What do we mean by environmentally sound ideas related to a decent standard of living? Those are, by the way, the sorts of questions that ought to be addressed in the universities, which now are not being addressed.

Also, as I have already mentioned, we have a full-employment act that should be applied now through an assessment of each community's needs, whereby each community performs a needs assessment program of its own to see how this particular community can be rebuilt, how this is to be accomplished in terms of practical projects to be undertaken.

This issue raises another point: Can there be a transformation of the military and refocusing of the efforts of scientists and technologists away from military production to civilian production? Here I think the answer is very complicated.

High technology workers and scientists are accustomed to working on difficult problems which more often than not have been tied to the national security state. Satellite development, nuclear bomb-making, precision weapons, and so on require great skill to create, develop, and manufacture. Whether the national laboratories will come up with a challenging alternate agenda remains to be seen. Surely some of these technological capabilities should be diverted to the cleanup of the massive toxic and nuclear wastes, a byproduct of decades of military production. But such activities are merely the beginning of how these industries can be converted.

H.F.: Getting back to the Pentagon, what function is the Pentagon serving now with regard to either facilitating or resisting disarmament? And could you respond to that by commenting on the Pentagon's Five Year Defense Plan for 1994 to 1999, which was leaked to *The New York Times* just a few days ago?

M.R.: The Pentagon planning document, as described in *The New York Times* report, is peculiar because it suggests that the United States should function as the sole remaining superpower, that no other nation should be in a position to challenge this superpower status, and that the United States must develop the military capacity to face down any particular nation or group of nations that might challenge our supreme position. Now this is basically a *Pax Americana* policy, and this position, historically, has always failed at least in modern times.

On its own terms, this kind of a plan is a terrible mistake for American life, American society, and for the world. Especially for American society it is a terrible error because it doesn't do anything to improve the living standards of the people of the United States. And it is a wildly expensive proposition for the United States. The assumptions of this plan are all wrong, that is, that the United States can or should be the policeman of the world, and should be the rational entity that decides and interprets the law for the world. Finally, it commits the United States to a continuous arms buildup and may force other nations to respond by committing themselves to an arms race, so it puts us right back in the soup.

This policy, as described in the leaked Pentagon document, establishes the principle that the United States will not be in a position to move the world toward a system of international cooperation, and the fundamental characteristic of development within the international system must be one of cooperation grounded in law, including a disarmament paradigm grounded in law. I think there will be a struggle around this Pentagon document and the development of the next stage of U.S. doctrine in international politics. It is one important reason to present a competing paradigm.

H.F.: The leaked Pentagon document leads us to an important question with regard to the conflict between movement toward a world order based on international law and disarmament and the reality of long-standing U.S. institutions that have functioned to thwart this movement. What will these U.S. institutions do if the society as a whole begins to demand disarmament? What will the Pentagon, for example, be likely to do in response to that?

M.R.: Well, the Pentagon has to be transformed. To the extent that the Pentagon would remain as a U.S. institution in the context of a world order grounded in disarmament and international law, it would remain to be prepared to defend the territorial borders of the United States, to assist the Military Staff Committee at the United Nations to develop a global peacekeeping and collective defense force. Once the imperial offense doctrine is off our collective backs, new systems of defense and ways of paying for it can then be considered.

H.F.: Let's keep talking for a moment about the conflict between disarmament and international law on the one hand and U.S. institutions on the other. You've just briefly outlined how the Pentagon would have to respond to your disarmament treaty. What about the Central Intelligence Agency and the National Security Agency and the rest of the U.S. intelligence community? What would happen to these agencies during implementation of a disarmament treaty?

M.R.: There is a contradiction between intelligence in a pragmatist sense, of openness, and intelligence in the sense of closed, covert intelligence. My view is that intelligence should be absolutely public, and that the C.I.A. and N.S.A. should now be transformed into a world library, that is, a world information system in which other nations would take part. That world information system would dedicate itself to questions and issues dealing with the environment, education, health, and to assuring that the disarmament process is in fact occurring. To the extent that we have a world satellite system under the operational control of the National Security Agency, this capability would become part of an international system of satellite observation, which would include the satellite capability of other nations as well, the product of which would be shared with the global community. Other nations would be invited to participate in a true system of intelligence-gathering where information and analysis would become shared and made public, and which would be used to benefit the world community, rather than used for the narrowly-defined interests of a single nation or bloc of nations.

Regarding covert operations, they are inherently, for the most part, by their nature, a violation of international law, and therefore we should have no covert operations. This is one reason why I propose in the treaty on disarmament and common security and in one of the chapters in this book that the operations sections of the intelligence agencies of every country be disbanded. That part of the C.I.A. that handles covert operations, the Directorate of Operations, would therefore be dismantled, as would the operations sections of the other intelligence agencies in the United States. The intelligence committees of the House and Senate would have to oversee this process and ensure that the United States was out of the covert operations business.

H.F.: Thus, the National Security Adjustment Act, which you have proposed and which would encompass much of what we have been discussing, would reverse and undo the National Security Act of 1947?

M.R.: That's right. The whole National Security Act of 1947 is to go, because it is predicated on a conflict/threat view of the world, and on containing or rolling back an enemy that now doesn't exist. We have to end a particular era of history, which was governed by very simplistic views of political reality. We need to move on. My fear is that if we don't understand that we have to move on to a whole different system of institutions and relations, we will move backwards to something similar to the periods prior to the First and Second World Wars, which would be an absolute disaster because it would mean the wider proliferation of nuclear weapons, modernizing of nuclear and conventional forces, no disarmament, extraordinary costs in order to do this, and the poor and disadvantaged in the world getting much poorer. Intelligence must yield wisdom and the knowledge that we need to improve our world. When it is closed and secret, it yields paranoia and not much else. Intelligence must be cross-examined through public inquiry. Information held by the few is just another form of monopoly.

H.F.: Let's assume that a disarmament project proceeds and as a result we have all of these disgruntled military and intelligence people in the United States. Do you think that our constitutional structures, specifically, civilian control over our military and intelligence institutions, would hold up to the political pressure involved in dismantling these institutions, and that we would be prepared to deal sufficiently with reactionary, possibly violent responses from rejectionist military and intelligence officials?

M.R.: There's always a problem and the possibility of extraordinary violence when you begin to shake institutions. It should be noted, however, that the transformation which occurred in Eastern Europe, and to a large extent in the Soviet Union, was done quite peacefully. And that what international law allows for is the legitimation of a world alternative which then is internalized in each nation.

So if the fight is going to come against such a treaty, it will come in my view before the transformation occurs. Once the process begins, and once you build in, as I hope I've built into this treaty proposal, massive involvement from people in terms of inspection, in terms of groups participating, in terms of journalistic oversight, in terms of leaders having to go on television every few months to talk about the process itself, the consequence will be to legitimate one direction and delegitimate another.

In the process of that delegitimation, if what you do is put those people up against the wall, that is, the military and intelligence people, and say, look, you have no role here at all, get out, and we hate you, and all we're going to do is to use the Nuremberg Principles against you, we would be committing a very grave error. I think the result would be a very terrible struggle. If on the other hand, we say that there's got to be a National Security Adjustment Act, which moves in this direction as we internalize the Nuremberg Principles, then it seems to me that what we are doing is setting a course for a more productive, more harmonious direction and wise policy. Many of the people in the military are not committed to war. They really are not. War is not their purpose. Their purpose is a sense of patriotism and protection. To the extent that factions within the military are committed to war, you often have people who are quite pathological. The areas where there might be disagreement among the people who are not pathological are the following areas: Will the National Security Adjustment Act protect the United States? Will a reconstructed National Security Act be better for our society than what is presently in place? And can nonoffensive defense protect a regenerated American society? I think the answer from the military, perhaps following their input with the expertise that many military officials will be able to bring to this process, will be yes, this approach can do all of those things, especially compared to our present course and what will come of this course.

H.F.: What will have to happen to the relevant international institutions in order to facilitate implementation of the disarmament program?

M.R.: I think that certain questions will have to be very quickly debated. I don't think, by the way, that this general disarmament program has to wait for comprehensive changes within the U.N. structure. Those institutions that would have to change in congruence with the disarmament program are the following. There has to be a clear change in the Security Council membership, and a clear change with regard to the veto. The veto now can be exercised by five nations in order to protect themselves, but other nations cannot do that. So there can be U.N.-sponsored intervention for the purposes of peacekeeping and collective defense, but under the system of centralized power in the U.N. Security Council, never a U.N.-sanctioned intervention in Russia, China, the United States, Britain or France.

We also need to have new members of the Security Council who are given long terms. It may very well be that the permanency of membership will have to be changed to ten to fifteen years. For example, and this is just an example, Nigeria, India, Japan, Brazil, and Germany would become long-term members for a ten or fifteen year term. The alternative would be to have bloc members, or regional members, and then these regions would be a mechanism for operating under the aegis of the United Nations to diplomatically solve problems. That's another change that would make a very big difference.

The second thing would be increased involvement by nongovernmental organizations in the decision-making process of the international system. For example, right now the political leaders of the world don't seem to know what they're doing. They're quite lost, given the real problems that the world is facing and what these leaders are doing to address them. Those in government whose job it is to help solve such problems usually look to the worst traditions of power politics for solutions. These leaders are operating under an inertial sense that what we did yesterday is what we will do tomorrow, even as the most profound changes occur. And so that means that there has to be greater involvement from nongovernmental organizations in the decision-making process in the international system, from the grass roots and from communities within nations that need an international presence and political voice, such as indigenous peoples.

The third thing that we need is a new kind of consciousness about the world in which we all live, and that kind of consciousness will come from a recognition that the twenty-first century must be different from the twentieth century. The question is, are we in a position now to accept certain new standards? Just as, for example, slavery was abolished as the dominant principle of the nineteenth century, we must for the twenty-first century abolish the twentieth century principle of war. And our U.N. institutions must reflect that need for change, and so must our notions of personal accountability and personal responsibility as individual citizens and nations.

H.F.: Well, looking to the twenty-first century and the renunciation of war in that not-so-distant future, do you endorse the idea of a new international treaty that would explicitly confirm the illegality of nuclear weapons as we have discussed? Furthermore, would you endorse proposals for the establishment of an international criminal court, which would give qualified individuals and nongovernmental organizations the legal standing to hold political leaders criminally accountable for violations of international law that constituted war crimes, crimes against peace, and crimes against humanity?

M.R.: I would be most interested in supporting the establishment of an international criminal court, as well as the internalizing of the Nuremberg Principles in domestic law. The question, of course, is what charter of laws would be used by the court, and how would jurisdiction be enforced? Regarding nuclear weapons, I view the existence and manufacture and deployment of these weapons, and their use and threat of use, as illegal. And I think that international law does indeed provide a great deal of legitimacy to the idea of disarmament. Having said that, it doesn't change the fact that we have to get rid of these weapons as quickly as possible, and the twelve-year disarmament period that is outlined in the treaty is the way that this could be done.

H.F.: What would the implications be for our own society, and for the world as well, if the Raskin Treaty or other similar treaties influenced by the Raskin Treaty were rejected?

M.R.: Things like this are not simply rejected once. The struggle will go on. This will go on, it will be improved by others as it opens up a new set of questions. The treaty is meant to be a catalyst. It's open for change as conditions change. It is meant, above all, perhaps, to change the frame of reference, to develop a far different paradigm of international relations.

Documents such as this, that is, documents of first principle, always get changed and I understand that. I don't want to be understood as being a one hundred percenter, that it has to be this or nothing. I do want to be understood as being very serious about the fundamental principles which underscore this treaty and which, I claim on the basis of the horrors of the twentieth century, should be adopted by our institutions. I am convinced that the war system that we have endured throughout the twentieth century is morally and legally comparable to the institution of slavery that our country endured throughout much of the nineteenth century, and that, like slavery, the war system must be abolished. The question of what kinds of institutions will replace the war system must still be debated and developed and worked on by your generation over the course of the next century. I hope that this work is a step forward in that discourse.

There is a final point to be made. I have been criticized from two quarters for developing this treaty. I have already discussed one of these criticisms—that developing a treaty outline is the responsibility of people in power, something for governments to do. But this criticism mistakes the role of intellectual policy work and citizenship, which must develop precedents for governments to follow, just as political organizing in a democratic society must frame the debates which are conducted inside and outside of government. It is only through such a dialectical, interactive relationship that we can expect to have systemic, positive changes and arrive at a sense of common good.

There is another level of criticism which at once is both evanescent but very serious. This criticism states that laws and regulations are preceded by changes of heart and the presence of affection among peoples and nations. Unless this prior change occurs, all the documents in the world and all the signatures of statesmen on treaties are ultimately irrelevant. It is also argued that change in social relations between peoples and nations is not derivative of treaties. This view mistakes several purposes of a model treaty. The first purpose of a model treaty such as this is to show that it can be done and that doing it relates to a tradition which is already part of the ongoing dialogue that humanity has had with itself to define what humanity is or should be. The Magna Carta, for example, is more than a piece of paper. So is the Declaration of Independence, the Universal Declaration of Human Rights, and the Charter of the United Nations. These documents are statements of human need and purpose that represented turning points in human understanding—beginnings of new chapters of history that rejected or supplanted the reactionary orthodoxy of previous eras.

The other purpose of this treaty is as an instrument of organizing, that is, something more than merely an existential antiwar wail. It is a means to show that people and nations are able to systematize a different and far more progressive path to societal and international organization. In other words, it is an attempt to link political imagination with political practice and the best aspects of international law.

Finally, I believe strongly that there is a spirit in reality and in these aspects of law that serve as an engine of social and political change among peoples. Thus, while it is apparent to me that a treaty on general disarmament and common security, a program of demilitarization, and the enforcement of personal accountability standards with regard to political leaders are all eminently reasonable and rational proposals, such a treaty outline and disarmament program, even aside from real-world implementation, possesses intrinsic intellectual value in that it challenges the fundamental assumptions of contemporary political discourse, which is grounded in military and power-oriented assumptions, that, quite frankly, are not rational or humane. One might respond and say that this notion is too Hegelian, with the ideal being more important than the material. But I respond to that by saying: Let's give disarmament a chance—first, within our intellectual models, second, within the world itself. The time has never been better to apply the idea of disarmament to the material world.

CHAPTER TWO

DISARMAMENT AND COMMON SECURITY
A DRAFT TREATY OUTLINE
Marcus Raskin

Chapter I
Basic Commitments and General Principles

Article 1

1. Each Party to this Treaty affirms its commitment to the Purposes and Principles of the United Nations as set forth in the Charter of the United Nations.

2. Each Party affirms its commitment to the Pacific Settlement of Disputes as required under Chapter VI of the U.N. Charter, and to the means provided for in Chapter VII regarding Action with Respect to Threats to the Peace, Breaches of the Peace, and Acts of Aggression.

3. Each Party shall refrain in its international relations from the threat or use of force against the territorial integrity or political independence of any state, or in any other manner inconsistent with the provisions of this treaty.

4. Each Party affirms its commitment to the principles of international law as established by the Hague Regulations of 1907, the Nuremberg Principles of 1946, and the Four Geneva Conventions of 1949 and their Additional Protocol I of 1977.

5. Each Party affirms its commitment to the principles of international relations expressed in the United Nations' Declaration on Principles of International Law Concerning Friendly Relations and Co-Operation Among States in Accordance with the Charter of the United Nations (1970).

Article 2

1. The Parties intend to achieve general disarmament and common security by the year 2008 through the implementation in good faith and in a spirit of cooperation the Program for General Disarmament and Common Security (hereinafter referred to as the Disarmament Program) specified in this Treaty. The Disarmament Program is divided into three stages of four years each, to commence as soon as possible.

2. The purpose of the Disarmament Program is to secure the peace by eliminating all weapons of mass destruction, including nuclear, chemical, and biological weapons, all offense-capable nonnuclear weapons as defined by the World Security Agreement, and all paramilitary, "low-intensity warfare" and "special warfare" forces and capabilities as defined by the World Security Agreement.

3. The Parties to this Treaty may retain nonnuclear, nonoffensive defenses to be configured as border guard, coast guard, and air-defense forces. The maximum capabilities of these forces shall not constitute a capability or threat to attack or invade the territorial borders of any other state. The maximum capabilities of these forces shall be defined by the World Security Agreement.

4. The Parties to this Treaty may retain internal security forces sufficient for the maintenance of internal domestic order in compliance with the Universal Declaration of Human Rights (1948), the International Covenant on Civil and Political Rights (1966), the International Covenant on Economic, Social, and Cultural Rights (1966), the International Convention on the Elimination of All Forms of Racial Discrimination (1966), the International Convention on the Elimination of All Forms of Discrimination Against Women (1979), the Declaration on the Elimination of All Forms of Intolerance and of Discrimination Based on Religion and Belief (1981), and the Convention Against Torture and Other Cruel, Inhuman, or Degrading Treatment or Punishment (1984).

5. The capabilities of the internal security forces shall not include prohibited weapons or forces as specified in Article 2, Section 2 of this Treaty. The capabilities of the internal security forces shall not exceed the maximum capabilities of the nonoffensive defense forces as specified in the World Security Agreement. The capabilities of the internal security forces shall be included as a capability for the purposes of defining each state's nonoffensive defense capability.

6. For the purposes of maintaining a collective self-defense force and a peacekeeping force under the command of the Military Staff Committee of the United Nations Security Council, the World Security Agreement shall

stipulate how each state may contribute to those forces according to the "separation of capabilities" principle.

7. All collective self-defense alliances, as well as all bilateral military cooperation arrangements, shall be modified to conform with the objectives of this Treaty and to facilitate implementation of the Disarmament Program.

8. Each stage of the disarmament process shall include assurances, inspection, and verification. The disarmament process shall move automatically from Stage One to Stage Two to Stage Three unless one of the permanent members of the United Nations Security Council and at least one-third of the Parties to this Treaty object to the automatic progression from one stage to the next.

Article 3

1. In Stage One, each Party shall reduce its strategic, conventional, tactical, and paramilitary forces by thirty percent. The Parties shall achieve in Stage Two a further reduction of these forces by forty percent. The Parties shall achieve in Stage Three a final reduction of these forces by thirty percent. The reductions in each stage shall be verified by a system of zonal inspection.

2. The United States and Russia shall initiate the disarmament process in consultation with the permanent members of the United Nations Security Council and ten additional nations selected by the United Nations General Assembly. All Parties shall participate in the Disarmament Program in Stage One to the extent that this stage applies to their military forces and to the category of weapons that they possess. The Parties to this Treaty that are parties to alliance arrangements shall begin their reduction of forces and weapons in Stage One as a group.

Article 4

1. The Parties shall establish an International Disarmament Organization (IDO). The IDO shall operate as the world's principal agency for ending the arms race and creating international security for all states, large and small.

2. The IDO shall operate according to the Purposes and Principles of the United Nations Charter.

3. The IDO shall develop means for assuring that the provisions of this Treaty are implemented fairly and without military advantage to one Party or group of Parties.

4. The IDO shall make special efforts to ensure that the quantum of world armaments and military forces are reduced in such a way that the

disarmament process does not give military advantage to any state or group of states over any other state or group of states. Special attention in this regard shall be given to Stage One and Stage Two disarmament of weapons, weapons systems, and forces that constitute force-projection, interventionist, and destabilizing capabilities. No state shall be required to disarm components of its border guards, coast guard, and air-defense forces as defined by the World Security Agreement until Stage Three of the Disarmament Program, and then only as required in Stage Three by the World Security Agreement.

5. The IDO shall ascertain the effect on the implementation of the Disarmament Program upon any state that is not a signatory to this Treaty. The IDO shall submit reports in this regard to the United Nations Security Council, the United Nations General Assembly, and the Parties to this Treaty.

6. When decisions of the IDO are disputed, they shall be resolved by the International Court of Justice.

Article 5

1. In the event of disarmament violations, as determined by the International Court of Justice or a special tribunal of five persons appointed by the Court upon the request of the IDO, the offending Party shall be penalized financially according to a system of fines established by the Board of Inquirers. The fine schedule shall be submitted to the United Nations General Assembly and Security Council for final adoption.

2. Revenues from fines, if any, shall be used to meet the operational costs of the IDO. Any funds in excess of operational costs shall be made available to the specialized agencies of the United Nations for international aid and development.

Article 6

1. Upon the recommendation of the IDO, the United Nations General Assembly, or upon its own recommendation, sanctions may be applied by the United Nations Security Council to a Party or Parties that violate one or more provisions of this Treaty.

2. Upon the recommendation of the United Nations General Assembly, sanctions may also be applied by the United Nations Security Council to a state that is not a party to this Treaty that violates one or more provisions of this Treaty.

3. Such sanctions may include those specified in Articles 41-47 of the United Nations Charter. Nonviolent sanctions may also be devised by the U.N.

General Assembly and implemented by the U.N. Security Council upon the recommendation of the International Disarmament Organization.

Article 7

1. Upon the entry into force of this Treaty, each Party shall cease all research on new weapons prohibited by this Treaty, and shall cease testing and improvement of prohibited weapons systems already developed or deployed. Each Party may continue to manufacture spare parts for prohibited weapons for no more than ten years from the date of the entry into force of this Treaty.

2. From the communities of the Parties, the IDO, with the cooperation of the United Nations, shall establish a registry of scientists, engineers, technologists, and laboratory and industrial workers.

3. Consistent with its internal constitutional processes, each Party shall amend its internal laws to ensure that there is a positive responsibility on the part of scientific and technical workers to refuse to engage in development, research, or experimental work on weapons of mass destruction, including nuclear, biological, and chemical weapons, the delivery vehicles of such weapons, other offense-capable weapons and their delivery vehicles, or on military space- and laser-weapons research. Professional organizations, worker associations, and labor unions are encouraged to formulate a modern Hippocratic pledge either of the following or a variant thereof: "I will not use my scientific, educational, or technical training for the purposes of weapons research, development, manufacture, and deployment that is violative of the provisions, rules and principles of the Treaty on General Disarmament and Common Security."

4. The definitions of "research," "development," "manufacture," "experimental," and "deployment," as well as the definition of "weapons of mass destruction" shall be determined on the basis of their usage in international law, scientific inquiry, and commercial manufacture.

Article 8

1. The Parties solemnly undertake to uphold the Treaty on General Disarmament and Common Security and comply with its provisions within the required timetable.

2. In the event that a Party or group of Parties is not able to implement a part of the Disarmament Program within the specified timetable, the Party or Parties shall inform the Board of Inquirers so that an alternative procedure may be found to accomplish the objectives of the Program.

Article 9

The Parties shall adhere to the following international agreements which shall be considered as integral parts of this Treaty:

(a) Protocol for the Prohibition of the Use in War of Asphyxiating, Poisonous or Other Gases, and of Bacteriological Methods of Warfare (1925);

(b) The Antarctic Treaty (1959);

(c) Treaty Banning Nuclear Tests in the Atmosphere, in Outer Space and Under Water (1963);

(d) Treaty on Principles Governing the Activities of States in the Exploration of Outer Space, Including the Moon and Other Celestial Bodies (1967);

(e) Treaty on the Non-Proliferation of Nuclear Weapons (1968);

(f) Treaty on the Prohibition of the Emplacement of Nuclear Weapons and Other Weapons of Mass Destruction on the Seabed and the Ocean Floor and in the Subsoil Thereof (1971);

(g) Convention on the Prohibition of the Development, Production and Stockpiling of Bacteriological (Biological) and Toxin Weapons and on Their Destruction (1972);

(h) Treaty Between the United States of America and the Union of Soviet Socialist Republics on the Limitation of Anti-Ballistic Missile Systems (1972);

(i) Any other treaties on international security or disarmament, such as START I and START II, that may be agreed upon before the entry into force of this Treaty, unless one of the permanent members of the Security Council or one-third of the Parties to this Treaty object to the addition of a particular treaty to the list.

Article 10

The Parties shall waive the right to make reservations to any particular part or article of this Treaty unless two-thirds of the other Parties accept the reservation.

Article 11

1. To facilitate inspection and verification each Party shall deposit an official declaration on the status of its armed forces within three months after the entry into force of this Treaty.

2. The United States and the nuclear powers within the Commonwealth of Independent States shall deposit their declarations with the IDO at the same time. The declarations shall include an authoritative accounting of personnel strengths, arms and equipment, industrial plants, military bases, establishments and facilities, and all other information which is relevant to the conduct of inspection and verification assignments.

3. Without limiting the generality of paragraph 2, the declarations shall include:

(a) the personnel strengths of naval, land, and air forces, and auxiliary forces;

(b) the number of conscripts and the Party's intention with regard to its draft law;

(c) the number of reservists that are available for recall to full-time or part-time service;

(d) the number, by category, of single atomic and thermonuclear weapons with their yield in kilotons;

(e) the number of multiple warheads, with their yield in kilotons, and the number of individual guidance systems;

(f) the number, by category, of delivery vehicles capable of delivering atomic or thermonuclear weapons at a range of 100 kilometers or greater;

(g) the number of locations of sites for launching these delivery vehicles;

(h) the number of rocket launching sites for peaceful purposes;

(i) the number of naval bases;

(j) the number of shipyards for building and servicing ships of war;

(k) the number of ships of war, by categories and types, including submarines and fleet auxiliary vessels;

(l) the number of aircraft by categories and types;

(m) the number of airfields and air bases with locations;

(n) the number, by category, of plants and facilities producing or servicing various types of military arms and equipment;

(o) the number of military and paramilitary training establishments;

(p) the number of weapons for land forces by categories and types;

(q) the number of proving grounds and firing ranges;

(r) the number of stockpiles of various categories of weapons;

(s) the number, by category, of laboratories engaged in research and development for military purposes;

(t) the quantity, by category, of various chemical, biological, and radiological weapons.

Article 12

Any declaration under this chapter shall indicate, with respect to any listed item that is located outside the territory of the Party making the declaration, in what foreign territory that item is located, and where geographically it is located within that territory.

Article 13

Each Party shall provide the IDO with the locations and times it will discharge members of its armed forces as required by the Disarmament Program. The IDO shall circulate this information to every other Party that has notified the IDO of its desire to observe such discharge.

Chapter II
The International Disarmament Organization, Its Staff, and the Board of Inquirers

Article 14

In the initial stages of organizing the IDO, the Parties to this Treaty, especially the militarily significant Parties, in addition to the United Nations, shall remain responsible, jointly and separately, for carrying out the objective of ending world insecurity caused by the arms race.

Article 15

Each Party shall be assessed for the expenses of the IDO according to a percentage contribution formula based on each state's share of world military expenditures averaged over the five years prior to the entry into force of this Treaty.

Article 16

1. A Director-General of the IDO shall be chosen by the Board of Inquirers for a tenure of six years.
2. The Director-General shall be assisted by Deputy-Directors-General who are expert in diplomacy, disarmament, international security, or other

fields of endeavor relevant to the implementation of the Disarmament Program.

3. The Director-General and the Deputy-Directors-General shall be entrusted with the appointment of staff and administration of the IDO.

4. The staff of the IDO shall be supervised by the Director-General.

5. The IDO shall be staffed by competent individuals from all nations. The IDO shall, as part of the Disarmament Program, conduct training and educational activities for its staff, inquirers, and inspectors, and provide them with adequate research facilities.

Article 17

1. Each Party agrees to appoint a senior national official and give him or her the power of direct communication with the Director-General of the IDO on technical matters.

2. The United Nations shall appoint a Deputy-Secretary-General-who will serve as liaison with the IDO.

3. The IDO shall operate in close association with the specialized agencies of the United Nations and shall seek advice, counsel, and staff, when necessary, from those agencies and other international agencies.

4. The IDO shall work closely with nongovernmental organizations and citizen groups in order to obtain international popular support for carrying out the terms of this Treaty.

5. The IDO shall negotiate an agreement with the International Atomic Energy Agency to employ the services of that agency when necessary.

Article 18

Each Party agrees to present to the IDO all information requested by the IDO relevant to compliance with the provisions of this Treaty.

Article 19

1. The staff of the IDO shall owe its primary loyalty to no government. It shall be politically independent and will, in its conditions of service, hold to the highest standards of integrity and technical skill. It shall specialize in settling disputes or conflicts over technical data or disagreements caused by language or cultural misconception. The staff shall be chosen without regard

to race, religion, sex, or age, and shall reflect, to the extent possible, wide geographical composition.

2. The staff of the IDO shall be instructed in procedures of verification, assurance, and inspection for at least six months prior to acting as independent investigators. Contracts for professional staff shall remain in force for a period of five years.

Article 20

1. The staff of the IDO, including the Director-General and the Deputy-Directors, shall not receive or seek instructions from any state. All discussions that take place between or among the Director-General, the Deputy-Directors, the IDO staff, and government officials are to be considered official discussions when they concern the Disarmament Program, and records of those discussions shall be kept by the IDO.

2. Each Party solemnly agrees to protect the integrity of the Disarmament Program by respecting the quasi-judicial functions of the Director-General and the IDO staff. Upon the request of the Director-General, a Party shall be obligated to facilitate the grant of its citizenship to staff members of the IDO desiring it and to their immediate families.

3. Governments which seek special favor with the IDO through bribery or by suborning its staff may be penalized, in ways proportionate to the transgression, by the International Court of Justice, or the special tribunal appointed in accordance with Article 5, Section 1 of this Treaty. Military force or the interruption of the Disarmament Program may not be used as a penalty for subornation.

4. Where possible, the IDO shall seek to identify procedural inadequacies within the Disarmament Program that might have unintentionally encouraged a Party to act irresponsibly or to seek undue influence.

Article 21

1. The IDO shall have the authority to hire consultants, call on research institutes, award contracts for specified jobs, and seek advice and counsel from nongovernmental organizations.

2. All such discussions shall be official and records of those discussions shall be kept by the IDO.

3. No individual, institute, or other organizational body shall interfere with the Disarmament Program or seek to corrupt the staff of the IDO.

4. Where such improper acts occur, the IDO shall inform the authorities of the state of which the alleged guilty party is a citizen or resident so that it may take appropriate legal action in accordance with its laws, including those laws enacted by that state to implement this Treaty.

Article 22

The Board of Inquirers shall have the following functions:

(a) to appoint the Director-General of the IDO;

(b) to appoint regional Deputy-Directors-General of the IDO;

(c) to recommend to the United Nations Security Council and General Assembly the fines to be imposed on states violating this Treaty and the punishments that ought to be assigned by Parties to other violators, in accordance with any regulations that may be adopted pursuant to this Treaty, the United Nations Charter, or U.N. General Assembly and U.N. Security Council resolutions;

(d) to fix the assessments and contributions of the Parties;

(e) to initiate, formulate, and approve all agreements with states Members of the United Nations, specialized agencies of the United Nations, and other international institutions that may be required for carrying out the objectives and terms of this Treaty;

(f) to adopt the same rules for the Chair of the Board of Inquirers that are followed by the Presidency of the United Nations Security Council;

(g) to meet in places other than where it is permanently located if the Disarmament Program would be facilitated thereby;

(h) to establish committees comprising consultants, specialists, and members of nongovernmental organizations to facilitate the implementation of the Disarmament Program;

(i) to supply interim reports on the implementation of the Disarmament Program to the Parties, the United Nations Security Council and General Assembly. It shall issue also special reports on technical aspects of verification, inspection, and assurance;

(j) to regularly use television, film, radio, and other means of communication to report to the world's people progress in the implementation of the Disarmament Program;

(k) to report to the Parties, the United Nations, and the international public at large on current research relevant to the implementation of the Disarmament Program.

Article 23

1. The Board of Inquirers shall consist of the permanent members of the United Nations Security Council, and thirteen other members elected by the United Nations General Assembly from among those states that are Parties to this Treaty. Five of the states shall be elected from a list of major powers other than the permanent members. The list shall be prepared by the General Assembly upon the entry into force of this Treaty, and shall be revised at twelve-year intervals.

2. Each member of the Board of Inquirers shall be elected for a term of four years. Terms shall be staggered. Each state member of the Board shall appoint a specially qualified person as its representative on the Board. The Board may prescribe the qualifications of these representatives.

3. The Board of Inquirers shall be responsible for the implementation of the Disarmament Program.

4. The Board of Inquirers shall involve nongovernmental groups, such as scientists, engineers, technologists, peace and disarmament groups, organizations of former military officers and personnel, women's groups, labor unions, and political parties to secure their participation in the disarmament process. In preparing its reports, the Board will take into consideration reports prepared and testimony presented by these groups.

Chapter III
Common Security and International Organizations

Article 24

1. The Military Staff Committee of the United Nations Security Council shall meet on a continuous basis with the special representatives of the Parties to this Treaty and of the IDO to fulfill its obligations to prepare a World Security Agreement, which shall stipulate the precise military configuration of the Disarmament Program. Once that Agreement enters into force, its implementation shall parallel the implementation of the Disarmament Program.

2. At the end of each stage of the Disarmament Program, the consecutive parts of the World Security Agreement shall be presented to the United Nations Security Council and General Assembly for debate, approval, and implementation.

3. The Military Staff Committee shall be responsible for the implementation of the World Security Agreement, and shall exercise for this purpose functions similar to those performed by the Board of Inquirers with respect to the Disarmament Program.

Article 25

1. Each Party shall contribute contingents of armed forces to a United Nations Peace Force that shall supplement the standing United Nations Collective Defense and Peacekeeping Force specified in Article 26, Section 1.
2. The primary emphasis of the United Nations Peace Force shall be highly technological and nonlethal. It shall explore the efficacy of various sublethal methods of maintaining the peace. The United Nations Peace Force shall be used for humanitarian purposes, such as assistance in response to natural disasters and the security of human rights, pursuant to the orders of the United Nations Security Council.
3. All uses of the United Nations Peace Force shall conform to regulations adopted by the United Nations Security Council, and shall be subject to the mobilization and field deployment decisions of the Military Staff Committee of the Security Council.

Article 26

1. The Military Staff Committee, under Article 43 of the United Nations Charter, shall organize and recruit a United Nations Collective Defense and Peacekeeping Force comprised of contingents from States Members of the United Nations.
2. Over the course of the three stages of the Disarmament Program all weapons, vehicles, and armaments shall be destroyed to the extent provided for in the Program. In the last stage of the Program, a Party may deduct from the percentage to be destroyed those weapons, vehicles, and armaments that are needed for its contribution to the United Nations Force, to the extent provided for by the regulations stipulated in the World Security Agreement.
3. No international organization, or collective defense or peacekeeping force shall retain, develop, or contract to be developed, weapons of mass destruction and terror weapons, nor shall it be permitted to secure the peace through plans and programs of terror, mass bombing, or other means that would violate the principles for the protection of noncombatants embodied in the Geneva Conventions of 1949 and the Protocols of 1977, or the principles specified in Article 32, Section 1 of this Treaty.

Article 27

1. The Military Staff Committee, in cooperation with the staff of the IDO, shall prepare for inclusion in the World Security Agreement rules governing ways to handle border incidents and plans for securing armed forces upon short notice from states Members of the United Nations, whenever necessary for the maintenance of international peace and security.

2. The World Security Agreement may authorize the Military Staff Committee of the United Nations Security Council, and the IDO, to make arrangements for border patrols in, including but not limited to, the Middle East, between China and Vietnam, the former Soviet Union and China, North and South Korea, Cambodia and Vietnam, the Republic of South Africa and its neighboring states, and Eastern Europe. The Military Staff Committee shall make prompt arrangements for the withdrawal of troops that have crossed another state's borders.

Article 28

From time to time, but at least every five years after the end of Stage Three, the Parties shall meet to discuss whether reductions in the nonoffensive defense forces retained may be made. They shall also discuss the further implementation of the World Security Agreement as a means of keeping the peace.

Chapter IV
The Three Stages of Disarmament

Article 29

The Parties shall agree that the armed forces and armaments of each of them that may remain after each stage shall be determined precisely in accordance with the provisions of this Treaty and the terms of the World Security Agreement.

Article 30

1. The Parties shall encourage independent measures of disarmament announced and executed by any state able to do so.

2. Any Party may act, either individually or together with other Parties, to reduce its armed forces and armaments in advance of the stages of the Disarmament Program. It shall not, however, be subject to inspection and on-the-ground verification until the time and period called for in the Disarmament Program.

Article 31

Within each stage, the reductions shall proceed on the basis of quantitative measures, unless otherwise agreed by all the Parties concerned. The categories for the disarmament process shall be:
- (a) space delivery vehicles and space objects, including lasers;
- (b) ballistic delivery vehicles with a 20-mile range or less;
- (c) ballistic delivery vehicles with a range greater than 20 miles;
- (d) airplanes with speeds of 1000 miles per hour or less;
- (e) airplanes with speeds greater than 1000 miles per hour;
- (f) nuclear warheads with a 20 kiloton explosive yield or less;
- (g) nuclear warheads with an explosive yield greater than 20 kilotons;
- (h) naval vessels;
- (i) artillery, including rockets;
- (j) tanks;
- (k) armored vehicles;
- (l) chemical, biological, and radiological weapons;
- (m) munitions;
- (n) uniformed full-time military personnel.

Article 32

1. At the beginning of Stage One of the disarmament process, the Parties shall take the necessary legislative or other measures to give effect in their domestic laws to the principles of international law recognized in the United Nations Charter, the Judgment of the Nuremberg Tribunal, and the Judgment of the Tokyo Tribunal, so that the destruction of innocent populations, the preparation for aggressive war, the use of terror weapons, or the use of force in the conduct of international relations in a manner inconsistent with the United Nations Charter shall qualify as a crime not only against international law but also against domestic law.

2. Such criminal provisions shall be in force as part of the domestic law of each Party by the end of Stage Three of the disarmament process.

3. The military codes of each Party shall establish the duty of its military forces to observe scrupulously the principles specified in Section 1 of this article.

4. As the Parties disarm, the IDO and the Military Staff Committee shall, upon request, instruct national military forces and others on the use of nonviolent techniques as a primary way of encouraging collective confrontation against any state or group in breach of this Treaty.

5. The United Nations and the IDO will encourage universities, law schools, institutes, and governments to prepare teaching, research, and informational materials to facilitate the implementation of this article.

Article 33

1. In accordance with Article 11 of this Treaty, the Parties shall, within one month after the entry into force of this Treaty, file the declarations containing the interim but comprehensive official inventories of all military equipment, a list of all industrial plants which manufacture military equipment in substantial amounts, the contract and requisition data, and military personnel lists. The inventories and lists shall not include the location of these weapons, plants, and forces. Such disclosure shall be made later to the extent required by the zonal disarmament procedure.

2. All Parties may amend the inventory and personnel lists throughout Stage One. In Stage Two the inventory and personnel lists may be amended twice. In Stage Three the inventory and personnel lists, which in that stage should include not only members of regular armed forces but also paramilitary and intelligence personnel (as specified in Article 45, Section 2), may be amended once.

Article 34

The Parties shall have a choice of two methods of zonal disarmament. They may choose:

(a) complete disarmament of a zone without any prior disclosure of the forces, military equipment, and industrial plants in that zone, followed by a verification of the fact of such disarmament; or

(b) presenting an inventory of the forces, military equipment, and industrial plants, followed by the verification of this inventory and by disarmament of such a percentage of these forces, equipment, and plants as required to comply with the provisions of the Disarmament Program for a particular stage or part of a stage. A Party may not change methods without the express consent of two-thirds of the Parties to this Treaty.

Article 35

In Stage One of the Disarmament Program, the Parties shall withdraw their forces, including their artillery, rockets, airplanes, and ground forces from areas where, because of individual or alliance policy, there is a danger of direct engagement with an adversary or the likelihood of creating or adding to regional instability. Wherever direct engagement exists between adversaries or potential adversaries, a process of "back-off" and confidence-building measures shall be completed in the first fifteen months of Stage One.

Article 36

The Parties shall designate depots at which weapons and war materials will be destroyed before inspectors of the IDO and invited nations. Citizen monitoring through nongovernmental organizations and citizen groups shall be encouraged.

Article 37

Nuclear warheads/charges shall be destroyed according to the following procedures:
 (a) Each nuclear warhead/charge shall be detached from its mode of delivery.
 (b) Its guidance system shall be destroyed.
 (c) The fissile material shall be removed from the warhead/charge and deposited.
 (d) The warhead/charge shall be physically destroyed.
 (e) IDO inspectors shall be present at the destruction of the warhead/charge.
 (f) The Parties shall be invited to witness the process of physical destruction.

Article 38

1. The fissile material shall be denatured as quickly as possible and placed under the custody of the IDO.

2. The IDO, through the Director-General and Board of Inquirers, shall publish an annual progress report on the denaturing of the fissile material.

Article 39

Thermonuclear warheads/charges shall be destroyed according to the following procedures:

(a) The atomic trigger shall be removed from the warhead/charge and denatured as quickly as possible.

(b) The warhead/charge shall be detached from its mode of delivery.

(c) Its guidance system shall be physically destroyed.

(d) Tritium shall be disposed of in an environmentally safe and sound manner according to agreed upon means.

(e) The remainder of the warhead/charge shall be physically destroyed.

Article 40

Ballistic missiles shall be destroyed according to the following procedures:

(a) The guidance system shall be physically destroyed.

(b) Fuel shall be removed.

(c) Toxic fuels shall be encapsulated by vitrification, concretization, or other means and disposed of by the disarming states with full concern given to the environment and human safety.

(d) Where there is any scientific doubt about the harmful effects of any fuel related to the delivery vehicle, it shall be destroyed or buried in a geologically stable area, or in an agreed upon manner that is environmentally safe and sound.

(e) The remainder of the vehicle shall be physically destroyed.

Article 41

1. A limited number of missiles may be maintained by the Parties for satellite surveillance during the implementation of the Disarmament Program. At the end of Stage Three of the Program, the Parties shall ascertain whether independent satellite inspection should be continued in order to reinforce the satellite and on-site inspection system of the IDO.

2. These missiles shall not be used without prior notification and examination by the IDO. Their launchings shall be public and journalists and representatives of citizen groups shall be entitled to witness them.

Article 42

1. All launching pads, silos, underground depots and platforms, and mobile and fixed launching systems, which can be used for storage or blast-off and which are capable of delivering nuclear weapons or other weapons of mass destruction, shall be demolished.
2. Launching and guidance systems for controlling such vehicles, including their equipment, shall also be demolished.

Article 43

Launching for peaceful purposes of satellites shall occur only after prior notification to the IDO. Such launchings shall be public and journalists and representatives of citizen groups shall be entitled to witness them.

Article 44

The Parties agree to destroy all antisatellite weapons, and to cease all research, development, manufacture, or deployment of space satellites capable of destroying other space satellites.

Article 45

1. The Parties agree to reduce the military personnel of their armed forces according to the terms of the Disarmament Program.
2. The Parties agree that, for the purposes of the Disarmament Program, "military personnel" shall mean the armed forces of a state including civilian employees with the armed forces who serve a military purpose. Paramilitary and police forces, and border and custom guards, who have been issued machine guns or other heavy weapons, are also to be considered as "military personnel."
3. Full-time cadre for the training and absorption of reserve forces shall be counted as part of the armed forces. Each Party agrees that it will reduce substantially its organized reserve forces by the end of Stage Three of the Disarmament Program.

Article 46

1. The Parties shall reduce and eliminate all naval ships, except those specifically permitted for defensive purposes under the terms of this Treaty

and the World Security Agreement. Naval ships shall be divided into two categories:

(a) those that are in storage at the time of the entry into force of this Treaty; and

(b) those that are part of deployable battle forces.

2. Each Party agrees that all ships other than those specifically permitted at the end of Stage Three shall be destroyed under the supervision of the IDO. The Board of Inquirers may allow the acquisition for peaceful commercial use of individual ships where military equipment has been removed from the vessel and destroyed, provided that the Director-General of the IDO has certified that the ship is no longer capable of military attack use.

3. Nuclear units shall be removed from military nuclear-powered ships. They shall either be destroyed or placed in the safe custody of the IDO. The Board of Inquirers may require IDO inspectors to be stationed on board nonmilitary, nuclear-powered ships.

4. A Party shall invite representatives of the IDO and the Parties to this Treaty and others to witness the destruction and dismantling of its ships and hulks.

Article 47

1. During the implementation of the Disarmament Program, the Parties shall refrain from activities at sea which may cause military tension or conflict, and shall refrain from engaging in forward strategies beyond sea lanes ordinarily used for international navigation.

2. To prevent naval incidents, inspectors from the IDO shall be authorized to board any naval ship of a Party and may cruise on it for a limited period, as determined by the Board of Inquirers.

3. In Stage Three of the Disarmament Program, the IDO shall be entitled to appoint one or more inspectors per vessel, but no more than six per vessel. On board, the inspector shall have inspection rights, diplomatic immunity, and access at appointed times to the ship's crew and officers and to the principal documents on board to an extent to be specified by regulations adopted by the Board of Inquirers.

Article 48

1. The Parties agree that they will reduce military aircraft in all categories during all three stages of the Disarmament Program: in Stage One by thirty percent of the inventory declared in accordance with Article 11; in Stage Two by forty percent; and in Stage Three by thirty percent.

2. Airplanes, guidance, and navigational systems, and other military instruments attendant to air warfare, shall be destroyed physically at depots assigned for that purpose. Such destruction shall be witnessed in accordance with Article 36.

Article 49

Destruction of chemical, biological, and radiological weapons shall be carried out by means to be determined by a panel of scientists and technologists chosen by the IDO or by the Parties.

Article 50

1. Inhumane weapons such as enhanced radiation weapons, maiming weapons such as napalm, and other weapons, which cause adverse long-term toxic effects to persons or land, are prohibited.
2. The Parties note with grave concern that the use of herbicides and defoliants may lead to ecocide. Weapons deliberately designed to produce adverse changes in the environment are prohibited.

Article 51

1. Research, development (including testing), production, use, and military planning for or in connection with possible use, are prohibited in relation to unnatural and inhumane weapons.
2. This prohibition applies to:
 (a) herbicides and defoliants;
 (b) enhanced radiation weapons, whether involving a nuclear explosive device or the spreading of pulverized nuclear waste by air or any means whatsoever;
 (c) weather modification of any kind whether it be rain, fog, hail, lightning, or severe storms;
 (d) climate modification;
 (e) electromagnetic radiation;
 (f) electrical behavior of the atmosphere;
 (g) interference with the ozone layer;
 (h) wide-arms fragmentation munitions;
 (i) fuel-air explosives;
 (j) napalm-follow-on controlled fireballs;

(k) viral or bacteriological poisoning of the food, water, or atmosphere;
(l) genetic modifications of viruses and bacterium for military purposes;
(m) electromagnetic mind-altering devices.

Article 52

Installations needed for the purposes of maintenance, repair, and manufacture of armaments shall be dismantled in Stage Three of the Disarmament Program. An exception is to be made, to the extent provided for by the regulations prepared by the Military Staff Committee, for the repair, maintenance, and manufacture of weapons that may be retained under this Treaty for the purposes of maintaining territorial defense forces, internal security forces, and for the forces to be contributed to the United Nations collective defense and peacekeeping forces.

Article 53

Industrial training and educational activities which are part of the maintenance, testing, and development of a prohibited weapon are prohibited.

Article 54

Leaders of militarily significant states shall report to their own nations at least twice a year on the importance of continuing the Disarmament Program. The biannual dissemination of such reports shall encourage maximum media coverage of the Disarmament Program.

Chapter V
Forces, Weapons, and Military Production Facilities to be Retained at the End of the Disarmament Process

Article 55

1. By the end of Stage Three, each Party to this Treaty shall retain only those weapons, forces, and industrial capacity necessary for the maintenance of its territorial defense and internal security forces as defined in the World Security Agreement, and for the fulfillment of its obligations, as defined in the

World Security Agreement, to the United Nations collective defense and peacekeeping forces.

2. The Parties agree that the remaining forces needed for the maintenance of territorial defense, internal order, and the maintenance of international peace, as specified in Section 1 of this article, shall be stationed in particular zones designated by the IDO at the beginning of each stage of the Disarmament Program.

Article 56

The Board of Inquirers, or the Director-General of the IDO, shall report to the United Nations Security Council any threat to or breach of the peace and shall recommend to the Security Council what action it should take under Chapter VII of the United Nations Charter.

Article 57

1. The Parties shall, in cooperation with the IDO or the United Nations, undertake regional and international arms discussions to end the export and import of armaments and war materials one year after the entry into force of this Treaty. Replacement parts may be bought and sold throughout Stage One of the Disarmament Program. At the end of Stage One an international arms trade conference shall be called under the joint aegis of the United Nations and the IDO to ascertain the means needed to assure that the arms assistance and arms replacement trade system will end at an early date certain.

2. Each Party shall inform the IDO about all arms and material which it has exported in the ten years prior to the signing of this Treaty or which were in transit at that date, and the destination of those exports.

3. Each Party undertakes to inform the IDO also of all arms imported in the ten years prior to the signing of this Treaty, or which were in transit to it at that date, and the sources of export.

4. The IDO shall encourage scientists, workers, journalists, and scholars to report information and findings they might possess on any aspect of the arms race and military assistance to the IDO and their respective governments.

Article 58

The information to be furnished by the Parties to the IDO shall include information as to licenses for the local manufacture of armaments from designs provided by an exporting country, whether the original designer or not, and the extent to which such licenses make an importing country self-sufficient in the manufacture of any particular armament. It shall also include the names of the persons, natural or juridical, involved in the licensing or manufacturing process.

Article 59

Each Party undertakes to amend its domestic law so as to ensure that the operation of this chapter shall give it no right to obtain in its courts damages or other remedy for international breach of contract.

Chapter VI
Verification, Inspection, and Assurance

Article 60

1. The Parties recognize that the Program for General Disarmament and Common Security provides an overall framework for ending the arms race and depends on building up common institutions and social relations of trust.

2. Each Party agrees that effective verification of this Treaty is important to achieve general disarmament and common security and undertakes to cooperate to this end with the IDO.

3. The IDO and the Parties shall, to the extent possible, rely on technical means of verification by satellites and other nonintrusive monitoring devices.

4. The Parties shall develop a system of assurance by challenge and response, to be followed, if disagreement persists, by verification. Joint or international projects of verification, assurance, and inspection, and of research related thereto, are encouraged between the Parties.

5. Any failure to comply with the obligations of the agreed upon Program for General Disarmament and Common Security shall be presented to the Board of Inquirers and, if necessary, reported by the Board to the United Nations Security Council for required action.

Article 61

1. On a biannual basis, through the media and by means of official proclamations, the political leaders of the Parties to this Treaty shall encourage

the citizenry to cooperate in the inspection, verification, and assurance process.

2. The IDO shall make arrangements for nongovernmental organizations such as research institutes and universities, and for international professional organizations that have networks of scientists and technical personnel throughout the world, to join in a public system of assurance, inspection, and verification. Such arrangements shall confirm the right and duty of these organizations to publish information pertaining to the implementation of the Disarmament Program, and to present this information to the IDO, the Parties to this Treaty, and the news media.

3. The Parties shall encourage universities, research institutes, and others to carry out studies, discussions, and transnational contacts to assure that the inspection and verification process is effective and does not lead to a verification system that is either too unwieldy, ineffective, or intrusive.

Article 62

1. In the first two stages of the Disarmament Program, the Party under inspection shall have the choice of deciding whether it is to be inspected by the IDO or those Parties commonly thought to be its adversaries. In Stage Three the inspection shall be conducted by the IDO.

2. In Stage One of the Disarmament Program assurance, inspection, and verification shall be arranged in three ways:

(a) by checking against inventory and personnel lists and ascertaining that what was to be dismantled and destroyed or disbanded has in fact been destroyed or disbanded (for instance, through direct on-site inspection at specified depots);

(b) through independent satellite capability under the control of the IDO, which shall be able to ascertain, through photography and sensor technology, the character and location of the forces of each Party. (See Article 63, Section 1.);

(c) through the testimony of nongovernmental organizations, scientists, and other sources of public testimony that are likely to provide information on the extent of the implementation by each Party of its duties under this Treaty.

Article 63

1. The IDO shall encourage joint and unilateral satellite inspection systems among adversaries and the Parties to this Treaty. Information gathered

through such means or through unilateral satellite inspection shall be made available to the IDO for examination, unless the states concerned agree otherwise.

2. In the presence of representatives of the United Nations, the IDO shall inspect the destruction and dismantling of weapons of mass destruction, strategic delivery vehicles, offense-capable conventional weapons and other prohibited weapons and forces as defined in the World Security Agreement.

Article 64

The Director-General of the IDO, in consultation with the Parties to this Treaty, shall establish Committees of Verification to assist the Board of Inquirers in the evaluation of all questions relating to verification of disarmament, including:

(a) the procedures to be used for verification in each category of weapons and military forces;

(b) the technical means of making these procedures effective and credible and facilitating their application;

(c) the areas and subjects of research necessary for ensuring that verification procedures are both effective and credible;

(d) the perfecting of verification by challenge and response.

Article 65

For the purposes of assurance, inspection, and verification the IDO shall have the following rights and duties:

(a) to require the maintenance and production of operating records concerning matters relevant to the Disarmament Program;

(b) to call for and receive progress reports from the Parties and, until technical inspection and verification satellite systems are perfected, it shall have the power to send inspectors into any area.

Article 66

1. The IDO shall send inspectors into, or station inspectors within, the territory of any Party, as directed by the Board of Inquirers. The IDO inspectors shall have access at all times to all places within designated zones, according to the particular stage of the Disarmament Program. They shall have continuous and permanent access to the seat of government. They shall have the data

and access to any person who, by reason of his or her occupation or special knowledge, works with material, equipment, facilities, personnel, financial expenditures, or any other matter bearing on the successful outcome of the Program.

2. Each Party shall direct its government officials to cooperate fully with the inspectors. These officials shall identify, and indicate the exact location of, all materials, equipment, facilities, records, and data that are subject to inspection during the stage of the Disarmament Program then in progress.

Article 67

1. The Director-General of the IDO shall inform, in writing, the Party that is to be inspected of the name, nationality, and background of each inspector proposed and shall transmit a written certification of his or her relevant qualifications. The Party concerned shall inform the Director-General within ten days of receipt of such a proposal whether it accepts the designation of the inspector. If so, the inspector is then designated as one of the IDO's inspectors for that Party and the Director-General shall notify the Party concerned of such a designation.

2. If a Party at any time objects to the designation of an inspector for that Party, it shall inform the Director-General of its objection. In that event, the Director-General shall propose to the Party an alternative designation or designations. The Director-General shall immediately report to the Board of Inquirers, for its appropriate action, any repeated refusal to accept the designations of an inspector where such refusal would impede the inspection and verification process, and where technical satellite inspection is deemed insufficient.

Article 68

1. The visits and activities of inspectors shall be so arranged as to ensure the effective discharge of their functions with the minimum possible inconvenience to the host and disturbance to the facilities inspected.

2. Transportation, lodging, and other services shall be provided by the Party under inspection.

3. The Parties agree that the IDO shall have full rights to install sensing and recording devices and communications instruments in zones that have become subject to inspection. These devices may be installed—where necessary—inside plants, and will be standardized types for all the Parties.

4. To the extent consistent with the effective discharge of their functions, the inspectors shall conduct their activities in harmony with the laws and regulations existing in the state under inspection.

5. No inspector or other staff member of the IDO shall disclose to any person whatsoever any industrial secret or other similar confidential information coming to his or her knowledge by virtue of his or her official duties.

6. Inspectors shall be granted the diplomatic privileges and immunities necessary for the performance of their duties.

Article 69

1. The Director-General of the IDO shall determine upon the basis of the reports of IDO inspectors whether:
   (a) the Party under inspection has performed its obligations under this Treaty;
   (b) the Party has seriously failed or omitted to perform those obligations; or
   (c) the Party while in arrears in the performance of those obligations is seriously and sincerely striving to fulfill these obligations.

2. The Director-General shall present a report to the Board of Inquirers which may contain recommendations, whenever necessary, with respect to remedial steps to be taken to carry out the terms of the Disarmament Program.

Article 70

1. Any Party, which suspects that an activity in contravention of this Treaty has been carried out, or is about to be carried out, may lodge a formal objection with the Board of Inquirers and the IDO. The Party against whom an objection has been lodged may respond and present an explanation.

2. Nongovernmental organizations and other groups may file with the Director-General information or evidence that may reveal noncompliance with the terms of the Treaty. The Party against whom an objection is raised may respond and present an explanation.

Article 71

1. Objections raised under either of the two sections of the preceding article shall be investigated immediately by a special Committee of Inquiry comprising five persons chosen by the Director-General of the IDO from a list prepared by the President of the International Court of Justice.

2. The Committee's report shall be presented to the Board of Inquirers for special remedial action, unless the investigation has disproved the complaint.

Article 72

1. The International Court of Justice may give advisory opinions on any legal question arising under this Treaty which is brought to its attention by the IDO. Its advisory opinions shall be delivered within three months of filing the request, and shall be published and made available to the public.

2. Any dispute concerning the interpretation or application of this Treaty may be referred to the International Court of Justice by any Party to this Treaty that is a Party to the dispute in conformity with the Statute of the Court, unless the Parties concerned agree to another mode of settlement. The time limit for the decision by the International Court of Justice shall be no more than six months from the date of the filing of the application that brought the dispute before the Court.

3. Each Party undertakes to propose to its legislative authorities during Stage Three of the Disarmament Program that it should be authorized to accept the compulsory jurisdiction of the International Court of Justice in any legal dispute to which it is a party, in relation to another Party to this Treaty that has accepted the same obligation at least one year prior to the commencement of the dispute.

Chapter VII
Industrial Plants and Economic Conversion

Article 73

1. For the purposes of inspection and verification, detailed information about industrial plants that produce armaments, as well as information about transportation centers (rail, land, air, or sea), shall be submitted by each Party to the IDO and the other Parties to this Treaty within one month after the entry into force of this Treaty.

2. The plant facilities include those that are:
 (a) devoted to the production of armaments;
 (b) plants and installations wholly or partly engaged in their repair and maintenance;

(c) plants, arsenals, laboratories, or installations engaged in the testing or experimental operation of armaments.

3. These provisions apply to both privately and publicly owned facilities.

Article 74

The manager, owner, members of the board of directors, and local labor union president of any plant belonging to a category specified in Article 73 shall sign an affidavit stating that military production, testing, experimentation, and shipping has ended in that plant in accordance with the terms of this Treaty. These affidavits shall be filed with the national government and the IDO, and shall be accessible to the public.

Article 75

1. IDO inspectors shall be entitled to investigate, on a spot-check basis, the condition of the various plants in order to verify that development, production, experimentation, storing, and testing of weapons has been terminated in accordance with the terms of this Treaty.

2. Journalists and others are encouraged to write about the implementation of the provisions of this Treaty relating to the prohibited plants or military facilities.

Article 76

1. The internal laws of the Parties to this Treaty shall be revised in order to obligate each industry partly or wholly involved in military contracts to file an economic conversion program.

2. The Parties are aware that economic and social dislocations may occur as a result of the disarmament process. Each of the Parties, therefore, shall make arrangements consonant with its own economic judgments to develop national, industrial, community, and worker conversion programs.

3. Both the IDO and the United Nations shall establish special units to conduct studies on economic conversion and shall assist states in economic conversion by providing any state requesting such assistance with economic data, international-assistance data, and additional assistance or data as may be required.

Article 77

1. The Parties agree that all plants wholly or partially involved in military construction shall be subject to the terms and stages of the Disarmament Program.
2. Machine tools and equipment designed for the production and maintenance of armaments shall be destroyed by the end of Stage Three, except when they are needed for the limited purposes specified in Article 55, Section 1 of this Treaty.

Article 78

Military academies may be maintained for the training of military personnel for the purposes specified in Article 55, Section 1 of this Treaty. Their respective course of study shall include training relating to the territorial defense mission, and to the U.N.-sponsored missions relating to collective defense and international peacekeeping.

Article 79

1. Each Party shall furnish full details of its military, paramilitary, and intelligence budgets and appropriations, including its plans to participate in the internationalization of intelligence-gathering and analysis, to the IDO. It shall give the IDO inspectors, specifically trained in financial verification, access to financial and budgetary records.
2. The Parties agree to reduce their military budgets and appropriations for military and paramilitary purposes simultaneously with, and in proportion to, the reductions in their armed forces and armaments.

Article 80

1. The Board of Inquirers shall submit an annual report to both the United Nations Security Council and General Assembly on the reductions of national expenditures which have been achieved by the Parties to this Treaty as well as the expenses of dismantling, destroying, or converting to civilian use, arms, armaments, industrial plants, and other military items.
2. The Parties shall submit to the IDO information required for the preparation of the reports to be made under Section 1 of this article, as well as

documents relating to defense budgetary planning, military procurement, weapons acquisition, and personnel projections.

3. The IDO shall prepare studies and make recommendations as to the use to which the savings resulting from disarmament might be put in aiding national economies, providing economic and technical aid to the developing countries, and stimulating world trade.

Chapter VIII
Miscellaneous

Article 81

This Treaty shall be subject to ratification by the Signatory states in accordance with their respective constitutional processes. Instruments of ratification shall be deposited with the United Nations Secretary-General, who shall notify the United Nations of each ratification. The Treaty shall enter into force when ratified by each permanent member of the United Nations Security Council and by two-thirds of the other states Members of the United Nations.

Article 82

Where a conflict exists between this Treaty and other treaties, this Treaty shall take precedence. In the case of a conflict between this Treaty and the Charter of the United Nations, the Charter of the United Nations shall prevail.

TREATY COMMENTARY

Article 1(1)

The Preamble of the Charter of the United Nations begins as follows: "We the peoples of the United Nations determined to save succeeding generations from the scourge of war, which twice in our lifetime has brought untold sorrow to mankind, and to reaffirm faith in fundamental human rights, in the dignity and worth of the human person, in the equal rights of men and women and of nations large and small . . . ."

The Purposes and Principles of the U.N. Charter are stated to be as follows:

Article 1(1): To maintain international peace and security, and to that end: to take effective collective measures for the prevention and removal of threats to the peace, and for the suppression of acts of aggression or other breaches of the peace, and to bring about by peaceful means, and in conformity with the principles of justice and international law, adjustment or settlement of international disputes or situations which might lead to a breach of the peace;

Article 1(2): To develop friendly relations among nations based on respect for the principle of equal rights and self-determination of peoples, and to take other appropriate measures to strengthen universal peace;

Article 1(3): To achieve international cooperation in solving problems of an economic, social, cultural, or humanitarian character, and in promoting and encouraging respect for human rights and for fundamental freedoms for all without distinction as to race, sex, language, or religion; and

Article 1(4): To be a center for harmonizing the actions of nations in the attainment of these common ends.

Article 1(2)

See U.N. Charter Articles 33-38, and 41-47.

Article 2(1)

Beginning in 1993, and given three to four years of good-faith negotiating for a final, globally agreed-upon draft of the treaty on General Disarmament and Common Security, the first stage of the disarmament process should be completed by the year 2000. The year 2000 is a millennial year, and thus, one might hope, a time of hope and goodwill. It will also be an important year psychologically, since people will be thinking about the massive changes that have occurred in the centuries gone by and that are to occur in the years ahead.

The three-stage approach to disarmament is borrowed from the McCloy-Zorin Principles. The Soviet Union in 1960-62 sought a five-year disarmament plan, while the U.S. plan sought a disarmament period of nine years. This treaty outline has scheduled a disarmament period of twelve years divided into three four-year stages.

Since the United States and the Commonwealth of Independent States have reached basic agreement on arms reductions in conventional and nuclear forces, these agreements may be incorporated into the treaty on General Disarmament and Common Security.

Article 2(6)

In order to fulfill the requirements of U.N. Charter Article 43, several states will be required to retain a military capability beyond that of its territorial defense forces, that is, its border guard, coast guard, and air defense forces. So that the permissible retention of forces for participation in a United Nations-sponsored collective defense or peacekeeping action does not corrupt the integrity of the disarmament accord, and does not pose an offensive threat within the context of the nonoffensive defense regime, this treaty specifies that the retention of forces be structured according to the "separation of capabilities" principle.

The implementation of this principle would require that the retained military capabilities be divided among nations and regions in such a way that no single country or region would retain a self-possessed interventionist capability. For example, in addition to its territorial defense forces, a country may be required to maintain a significant air-lift capability for use in a future U.N.-sponsored action. However, that country would be prohibited from maintaining any other capability or capabilities that might, when combined with its airlift capability, constitute an offensive military threat as perceived by its neighbors. This "separation of capabilities" approach for retaining U.N. enforcement action forces would be applied to each of the retained capabilities as established in the World Security Agreement.

Although U.N.-available forces would be based on the territory of various states, these forces would be under the command of the Military Staff Committee of the United Nations, and all equipment, personnel, and operating expenses would be paid for by the United Nations.

Article 2(7)

All Parties to the treaty on General Disarmament and Common Security shall formally incorporate the terms of the treaty into their security arrangements, including those security arrangements developed before, during, and after implementation of the Disarmament Program.

Article 2(8)

The disarmament process as a means to change international relations has to date not been sufficiently explored. There is evidence to suggest that if disarmament becomes a continuous and cumulative process it will alter international enmities.

Article 3(1)

Zonal inspection is discussed in Article 34.

Article 4(1)

The McCloy-Zorin Principles state, as in this treaty, that the International Disarmament Organization (IDO) will "implement control over and inspection of disarmament." The IDO for McCloy-Zorin was to be "created within the framework of the United Nations." Similarly, the IDO in this treaty will work closely with the United Nations. The responsibilities of the IDO will supplement the role of the United Nations, since the United Nations, in contrast to the IDO, was not founded exclusively for the purpose of achieving arms control or disarmament.

Article 4(3)

The execution of the Treaty's provisions by the IDO shall be based upon quantitative, technical, military, and scientific judgments that are consistent with the provisions of this treaty.

Obviously, the successful implementation of a global agreement on general disarmament and common security, given the nature of such an agreement, is dependent upon the commitment of each militarily significant state. Less significant military powers and smaller states would be more inclined to commit to the agreement once they are convinced of the commitment of the more significant military powers to disarmament, and understand that the treaty does not constitute a pretext for preventing lesser powers from acquiring weapons and capabilities already possessed by the greater powers.

Article 5(1)

This article seeks to establish a means for maintaining the integrity and viability of the treaty in the face of violation(s), since violation(s) of the treaty do(es) not necessarily constitute abrogation or alteration of the treaty, or cessation of the disarmament process.

If for some reason the payment of fines cannot be legitimately applied as payment for costs incurred by the disarmament process, or in the event of surplus funds within a given fiscal year, the payment of fines may be applied to a U.N.-sponsored economic development program. The priority remains, however, to secure sufficient institutional funding of the disarmament process to ensure that the commitment to implementing the provisions of the Disarmament Program becomes a staple of international life.

Article 7

Because the qualitative arms race begins with weapons research, the weapons laboratories that conduct research, design, testing, development, or manufacturing of weapons and weapons systems prohibited by this treaty shall be permanently closed down.

Article 8(1)

Prompt completion of treaty obligations is important to avoid imbalances which can cause political instability.

Article 8(2)

This exception clause allows for adjustments in the technical procedures of disarmament.

Article 9

(a) This agreement, which was signed on June 17, 1925 in Geneva, Switzerland, prohibits the use of asphyxiating, poisonous or other gases, and of bacteriological methods of warfare. The ratified treaty was deposited in France by the Soviet Union on April 5, 1928, and by the United States on April 10, 1975.

(b) The ratified treaty was deposited in Washington, D.C. on November 2, 1960 by the Soviet Union, and on August 19, 1960 by the United States. The treaty states, in part, that "it is in the interests of all mankind that Antarctica shall continue forever to be used exclusively for peaceful purposes and shall not become the scene of international discord."

(c) Although official efforts to achieve a test ban treaty began in May 1955, the seemingly insurmountable problem of verification (or at least a system of verification agreeable to all parties) prevented an agreement on a comprehensive test ban (CTB). In July 1963, Premier Khrushchev proposed banning nuclear tests in areas where verification was not in dispute, namely, in the atmosphere, outer space, and under water. The subsequent treaty was deposited in Washington, London, and Moscow by the Soviet Union and the United States on October 10, 1963. Article 1 of this treaty states:

> Each of the Parties to this treaty undertakes to prohibit, to prevent and not to carry out any nuclear test explosion, or any other nuclear explosion, at any place under its jurisdiction or control:
> (1) in the atmosphere; beyond its limits, including outer space; or under water, including territorial waters or high seas; or
> (2) in any other environment if such explosion causes radioactive debris to be present outside the territorial limits of the State under whose jurisdiction or control such explosion is conducted . . . .

It should be noted as well that the test ban treaty calls for security and general disarmament as the stated policies of the signatories.

(d) This "non-armament" treaty is modeled somewhat on the Antarctica treaty. The ratified treaty was deposited in Washington, London, and Moscow by both the United States and the Soviet Union on October 10, 1967. The treaty declared that "[t]he exploration and use of outer space . . . shall be carried out for the benefit and in the interests of all countries, irrespective of their degree of economic or scientific development, and shall be the province of all mankind." Part of Article 4 of this treaty is reprinted below:

> State Parties to this Treaty undertake not to place in orbit around the Earth any objects carrying nuclear weapons or any other kinds of weapons of mass destruction, install such weapons on celestial bodies, or station such weapons in outer space or in any other manner.

(e) The ratified treaty was deposited in London, Washington, and Moscow by both the United States and the Soviet Union on March 5, 1970. As summarized in *Arms Control and Disarmament Agreements,* the Non-Proliferation treaty is designed to

> prevent the spread of nuclear weapons; provide assurance, through international safeguards, that the peaceful nuclear activities of states which have not already developed nuclear weapons will not be diverted to making such weapons; promote, to the maximum extent consistent with the other purposes of the treaty, the peaceful uses of nuclear energy through full co-operation—with the potential benefits of any peaceful application of nuclear explosion technology being made available to non-nuclear parties under appropriate international observation; express the determination of the parties that the treaty should lead to further progress in comprehensive arms control and disarmament measures.

(f) The ratified treaty was deposited in Moscow, London, and Washington by both the Soviet Union and the United States on May 19, 1972. Parties to the treaty agreed in Article 1

> . . . not to implant or emplace on the seabed and the ocean floor and in the subsoil thereof beyond the outer limit of a seabed zone . . . any nuclear weapons or any other types of weapons of mass destruction as well as structures, launching installations or any other facilities specifically designed for storing, testing or using such weapons.

(g) This treaty eliminates the entire class of chemical and biological weapons, unlike the Geneva Protocol of 1925 which prohibited the use of biological and chemical weapons, but not production and stockpiling. The ratified treaty was deposited in London, Washington, and Moscow by both the United States and the Soviet Union on March 26, 1975. Article 1 is reprinted below:

> Each State Party to this Convention undertakes never in any circumstances to develop, produce, stockpile or otherwise acquire or retain: (1) Microbial or other biological agents, or toxins whatever their origin or method of production, of types and in quantities that have no justification for prophylactic, protective or other peaceful purposes; (2) Weapons, equipment or means of delivery designed to use such agents or toxins for hostile purposes or in arms conflict.

(h) This treaty sought to prevent the development or deployment of anti-ballistic missile (ABM) systems. One site in each country was allowed to be defended against ballistic-missile attack with an ABM system. The treaty was signed in Moscow on May 26, 1972 by the United States and the Soviet Union.

Article 10

As a general rule in international law a nation has the right of reservation to any particular segment of a treaty it finds objectionable. However, the type of treaty outlined here would not favor such sovereign flexibility because of the interrelated and interdependent nature of such a treaty.

Article 11(1)

Should the IDO exist before declarations on the state of armed forces? The problem in formal terms is that the IDO is created by this treaty. The IDO in its skeletal form could accept the declarations and then within six months verify the accuracy of each declaration through non on-site means.

Article 11(3)

Items (a) through (t) are meant to detail the universe of personnel, weaponry, and systems that need to be disarmed or demilitarized.

Article 12

This clause is intended to guarantee that no country will benefit by sending its military hardware out of its country (perhaps to a militarily insignificant country) to prevent detection.

Article 13

The demobilization of forces will be accomplished in an orderly and systematic way. This article concerns only active (or uniformed) military personnel.

Article 14

Criteria for defining "militarily significant" will be established by negotiation through the U.N. Security Council with the advice of the General Assembly.

Article 15

The nations which invested most heavily in their military establishments will be expected to make the largest contribution for carrying out the terms of this treaty and for financing the IDO budget.

Article 16(1)

The six-year term is chosen because it is approximately midway through the twelve-year disarmament process, a proper time for reevaluation of personnel.

Article 16(4)

The Director-General has primary responsibility for the operations of the staff under the Board of Inquirers.

Article 16(5)

The staff members of the IDO and the Board of Inquirers should be highly skilled professionals drawn from a wide number of different countries, and should be competent in a number of diverse but relevant fields. Training grants, provided by foundations or participating countries, and dispensed to the United Nations University, to other selected universities, and to selected nongovernmental organizations, should be established now so as to provide the IDO and the Board of Inquirers with highly qualified individuals at the outset.

Article 17(1)

In the United States the person appointed would most likely be the Director of the Arms Control and Disarmament Agency, since the director of that agency is officially the chief adviser to the President on issues related to arms control and disarmament.

Article 17(2)

There is, in the United Nations, an Under Secretary-General for Disarmament. The presently small secretariat will have to be expanded substantially.

Article 17(5)

The International Atomic Energy Agency (IAEA) came into force in 1957 with the objective, according to its Charter, of accelerating and enlarging the use of atomic energy for "peace, health, and prosperity throughout the world," and to "ensure, so far as it is able, that assistance provided by it or at its request or under its supervision or control, is not used in such a way as to further any military purpose." The IDO shall work closely with the IAEA.

Article 18

It is the obligation of each Party to this treaty to ensure the dissemination or release of information relevant to its compliance with the provisions of this treaty. The Board of Inquirers, in conjunction with the signatories, will establish procedures for the dissemination and release of information relevant to compliance with the provisions in this treaty.

Article 19(1)

The United Nations University may be one of the educational institutions best suited to provide the IDO with independent, well-qualified staff. According to its Charter, the United Nations University is to involve "an international community of scholars, engaged in research, post-graduate training and dissemination of knowledge in furtherance of the purposes and principles of the Charter of the United Nations."

Article 20(1)

The staff of the IDO shall take instructions only from the Director-General of the IDO.

Article 20(3)

Violations of the treaty do not necessarily reflect an intention to abrogate the treaty, and shall not necessarily be treated as such. However, penalties commensurate to transgression will be determined by the International Court of Justice.

Article 20(4)

This provision allows for correction or modification of the technical procedures which might cause a nation to cheat.

Article 21(1)

Because so much expertise and interest lies in nongovernmental communities, the IDO will need the help of different communities to do its work.

Article 22

(a) The Director-General of the IDO shall work closely with the United Nations Secretary-General;
(b) These are to be people with technical and diplomatic skills;
(c) The Board of Inquirers has recommending or advisory power. Historically, except in mixed claims commissions, fines have not been used, although reparations are rewarded after a war. The fine system is found in the municipal law of Western nations. The "direct use of force" decision is one that shall be made by the U.N. Security Council and not the IDO;
(d) Assessment shall be made according to standard U.N. procedures;
(e) The IDO shall be the central body that implements a multilateral disarmament program;
(f) The reporting requirement also emphasizes the IDO's ties to the United Nations structure.

Article 23(1)

The thirteen other members chosen by the General Assembly are to be from "militarily significant" countries. At the 1962 Disarmament Conference, eighteen countries were considered "militarily significant." Criteria used to define "militarily significant" shall be established by negotiation through the Security Council with advice from the General Assembly.

Article 24

The Military Staff Committee's (MSC) only task is to examine from a military standpoint Article 43 of the U.N. Charter. In 1948, the MSC presented to the Security Council a forty-one article draft proposal outlining general principles which would govern the organization and use of the United Nations forces. The MSC also issued a draft report specifying the exact composition of this force. Neither report gained the unanimous support of the five delegations to the MSC. When presented to the Security Council, the reports were not unanimously supported there either.

Although the MSC still meets every other week, it has done nothing of substance since the 1948 deadlock over Article 43. The most significant and stubborn disagreement concerning the principles governing the U.N. forces concerned Article 11, "Contribution of Armed Forces by Member Nations." Here, China, France, Britain, and the United States argued that "each of the five Permanent members of the Security Council [should] make a comparable, initial, overall contribution to the Armed Forces [that] differ widely as to the strength of the separate components: land, sea, and air." In contrast, the Soviet Union argued that the "Permanent Members of the Security Council shall make available armed forces (land, sea, and air) on the Principle of Equality . . . ."

Article 32

Extracts from the Charter of the International Military Tribunal at Nuremberg are reprinted below:

Article 6: The Tribunal established by the agreement referred to in Article 1 hereof for the trial and punishment of the major war criminals of the European Axis countries shall have the power to try and punish persons who, acting in the interests of the European Axis countries whether as individuals or as members of organizations, committed any of the following crimes:

The following acts, or any of them, are crimes coming within the jurisdiction of the Tribunal for which there shall be individual responsibility:

(a) Crimes against peace: Namely, planning, preparation, initiation of international treaties, agreements or assurances, or participation in a common plan or conspiracy for the accomplishment of any of the foregoing;

(b) War Crimes: Namely, violations of the laws or customs of war. Such violations shall include, but not be limited to, murder, ill treatment or deportation to slave labor camps or for any other purposes of civilian populations of or in occupied territory, murder or ill treatment of prisoners of war or persons on the seas, killing of hostages, plunder of public or private property, wanton destruction of cities, towns or villages, or devastation not justified by military necessity;

(c) Crimes against Humanity: Namely, murder, extermination, enslavement, deportation, and other inhumane acts committed against any civilian population, before or during the war, or persecution on political, racial or religious grounds in execution of or in connection with any crimes within the jurisdiction of the Tribunal, whether or not in violation of the domestic law of the country where perpetuated.

Leaders, organizers, instigators and accomplices participating in the formulation or execution of a common plan or conspiracy to commit any of the foregoing crimes are responsible for all acts performed by any persons in execution of such plan.

Article 32(2)

Incorporation of the Nuremberg Principles into the domestic law of the Parties to this treaty is an essential aspect of the treaty's enforcement mechanism.

Article 33(1)

Study groups of defense industrial managers in the militarily significant states either among themselves or under the aegis of the United Nations would need to meet to plan procedures and methods of inventory of military equipment and materiel. A common inventory and notation system would be useful.

Article 33(2)

The assumption here is that statistical error or inability to account for all weapons at any one time may occur. The approximation theory of science is applicable here.

As each side moves from statistical or abstract reporting to empirical reporting, the inventory lists will become more refined.

Article 34

The two methods of zonal disarmament offered here present two ways to achieve the same objective. The second is preferable but more time consuming; the first allows for more secretive societies to do their own disarming, followed by verification to ensure that the whole zone has been disarmed, thereby not involving the three-stage percentage cut back. (See Louis B. Sohn, "Progressive Zonal Inspection: Basic Issues," in Seymour Melman, ed., *Disarmament: Its Politics and Economics,* American Academy of Arts and Sciences, Boston, Mass., 1962.)

Article 35

By withdrawing forces from areas of conflict or potential conflict (such as the border between North and South Korea), or by setting up military zones of distance, the chances of regional conflict disrupting the disarmament process will be diminished.

Article 36

Inventory maps at the proper time would be made available to the public through the United Nations or the IDO.

Articles 37-40

These articles could be combined into one, more general article. The article combining articles 37 through 40 might read as follows:

Nuclear weapons and their launchers should be destroyed with IDO inspectors and citizens as witnesses in such a manner that:
    (a) no vital component could be reassembled for use;
    (b) dangerous materials would be placed under the safeguard of the IDO which would find environmentally safe methods to guard or dispose of them;
    (c) this disposal would have to meet with the approval of the Parties to this treaty.

There are several difficulties with the specifics of articles 37-40 as they currently stand. With regard to Article 37, the trigger must be disarmed prior to removing the fissile material. It needs to be established in what sort of container and where the fissile material should be deposited. With regard to Article 38, a bureaucratic question emerges as to whether the IAEA should receive the fissile material rather than the IDO. It may be enough to have the IDO contract with the IAEA for its services, thereby utilizing the expertise and experience of the IAEA. With regard to Article

39, unless the treaty bans nuclear energy, U235 and plutonium will continue to be produced; thus taking fissionable material from weapons and disposing of it will not prevent the acquisition of fissionable material. One last point: Because we do not know exactly how the Chinese build their nuclear weapons, it may be risky to delineate exactly the steps for dismantling weapons.

Article 41

The purpose of this article is to assure continued satellite production for peaceful and security purposes. This article assures the involvement of the IDO in satellite surveillance.

Article 42

This article is problematic. For commercial, communications, and scientific reasons, we cannot expect people to give up the use of space. However, any launching pad, silo, etc., can be used for either peaceful or military purposes, and there is no way to determine (without on-site inspection prior to and during blast-off) exactly what is being launched. Some comprehensive system of inspection must be established, since a space shuttle or a Boeing 747 is as capable of carrying nuclear weapons as a B-52 bomber. Spot inspections and notification may need to be part of the policing of launching sites as well as designating specific sites for launches.

Article 43

Satellites shall be launched only after prior inspection by the IDO. Only through such inspection will it be possible to verify the peaceful use of the object to be launched. Limiting the number of launching sites will make inspection easier.

Article 46(3)

Nuclear units refer to the nuclear weapons systems or bombs on a ship.

Article 46(4)

The destruction of these ships should be accompanied by as much fanfare as their creation and should be witnessed by representatives of as many nations as possible.

Article 48(1)

Aircraft should be divided into three categories: strategic, tactical, and defensive. Planes that are deemed by the World Security Agreement to be defensive may be retained.

Article 48(2)

One way to implement this section would be for each state to publicly propose a method of destroying their instruments and weapons. The proposed method would be acceptable and implemented barring objections from other parties to this treaty.

Article 49

The destruction of chemical, biological, and radiological weapons must be environmentally safe, even though this is a difficult process. The Convention on the Prohibition of the Development, Production and Stockpiling of Bacteriological (Biological) and Toxin Weapons (1975) does not specify how these weapons would be destroyed. The only article that directly addresses the destruction of these weapons, Article II, is reprinted below:

> Each State Party to this Convention undertakes to destroy or to divert to peaceful purposes, as soon as possible but not later than nine months after the entry into force of the Convention, all agents, toxins, weapons, equipment and means of delivery specified in Article I of the Convention, which are in its possession or under its jurisdiction or control. In implementing the provisions of this article all necessary safety precautions shall be observed to protect people and the environment.

Article 50(1)

Although all weapons are inhumane, some are more cruel and inhumane than others. Weapons which cause unnecessary suffering and can only be used indiscriminately should be considered militarily excessive and illegal.

Maiming weapons include: incendiary weapons, such as napalm and white phosphorous, cause unnecessary suffering and are generally used indiscriminately (as in terror bombing); dum-dum bullets and high velocity on-impact rifles—such as the M-16—are unnecessarily cruel. Weapons which have a long-term toxic effect on human beings and the environment—such as Agent Orange—would also belong to this category. It is time to inventory nonnuclear weapons to ascertain their effects on noncombatants. A start in this direction was made in the 1977 Protocol for the Protection of Non-Combatants.

Article 50(2)

Defoliants and herbicides, when used on a massive scale, as in Vietnam by the United States, destroy crops (thereby denying food to humans and domestic animals) and forests (thereby denying food and shelter to wildlife). The delicate ecosystem of South Vietnam will take at least 100 years to return to its normal, pre-war state. (See Arthur H. Westing, "Indochina: Prototype of Ecocide," in *Air, Water, Earth, Fire: The Impact of the Military on World Environmental Order,* International Series no. 2, Sierra Club, May 1974.)

Article 52

When an installation is integral to the operation of the weapons scheduled to be destroyed, the installation shall be closed at the same time that the weapons are destroyed.

Article 53

The purpose of this article is to disband the infrastructure that supports weapons systems. This article could pose First Amendment problems in the United States. The treaty intention, however, is to interrupt prohibited government-sponsored activities and contracts.

Article 54

The purpose of this article is to establish and ensure a system of information dissemination and accountability between the leaders of the militarily significant states and their public constituents.

Article 59

This article refers specifically, but not exclusively, to arms contracts that are ended by a state or any other party, by signing this treaty. In other words, there can be no domestic or international breaches of weapons contracts once the treaty is signed.

Article 61

One of the assumptions of this treaty outline is that networks of scholars and technical people will work together transnationally to implement this treaty. Myrdal in *The Game of Disarmament* outlines how this system of involvement could work.

Article 64

No single system of verification should be relied upon for verifying the disarmament requirements of this treaty. It is only by implementing a number of different modes of verification that reasonable people may arrive at a working or common-sense definition of verification.

Article 65

The IDO retains the authority even after assurance systems are perfected to inspect any area according to the time schedule of the treaty.

Article 67

The purpose of articles 67-72 is to present a "full faith" picture of inspectors so that the host nation (that is, the nation being inspected) will know who is on its territory. The host nation will become a part of the verification and inspection process.

A State's objection to an inspector does not necessarily signify that that State is guilty of treaty violations. The State being inspected may fear commercial espionage, or seek to hide an accident or some inefficiency. However, repeated refusals to cooperate with inspectors will be interpreted as efforts to obscure possible treaty violations, and sanctions as described in the treaty may be applied to the host nation.

Article 68(1-6)

Administrative guidebooks governing the authority of on-site inspectors and the rights of host nations will have to be prepared by the IDO and the host nations.

There is no other way for an inspector to travel except by relying on at least some of the transportation services of the host nation, or of citizen's groups within the host nation. It is in the host nation's interest to provide or facilitate these services.

This section raises the question of intrusion, patent rights, and property rights. The standardized sensing and recording devices should be manufactured under the auspices of the IDO to reduce the incidence of abuses. This is important since the installation of these devices may at times be a contentious issue between inspectors and host nations.

When the laws of a state conflict or prohibit the "effective discharge" of the IDO inspection, the internal laws of the state shall yield to the treaty provisions. However, an appeals procedure should be established.

The legitimate tasks of inspectors do not include the acquisition and use of information for the purpose of selling or reporting such information to other nations. The authority of the IDO to verify the treaty, as well as its obligation to keep non-verification-related information confidential, is critical. This is especially important in

Western nations where there are great concerns regarding the integrity of industrial secrets, patents, etc. Nonetheless, the IDO shall have access to industrial plants and laboratories, despite objections of the host nation, if IDO inspectors determine that such access is essential to the verification of the treaty.

Inspectors shall be given the same rights and privileges accorded to diplomats. However, violations of the duties and obligations of IDO inspectors by an IDO inspector shall result in the dismissal of the inspector, following appeal if such an appeal is sought by the indicted inspector. Maintenance of the integrity of the IDO inspection system is of paramount importance to credible verification of the treaty.

Article 70

This article means to involve citizens groups and nongovernmental organizations in the disarmament and verification process. The opinions and findings of such groups and organizations shall be made available to the news media and shall be given serious consideration by IDO officials.

Article 72

The U.N. Charter states (article 96[1]) that "[t]he General Assembly or the Security Council may request the International Court of Justice to give an advisory opinion on any legal question." Article 96(2) also states that "[o]ther organs of the United Nations and specialized agencies, which may at any time be so authorized by the General Assembly, may also request advisory opinions of the Court on legal questions arising within the scope of their activities."

Article 74

This article seeks to extend the responsibility for disarmament verification to personnel within industrial and economic sectors, where military production takes place.

Article 75

Journalistic oversight is essential to the verification process. This article means to ensure the rights of journalists to access to information relevant to the disarmament and verification process, and the rights of journalists to publicize such information.

Article 78

Military academies would be permitted to continue functioning following a reorientation of curriculum that focuses exclusively on implementation of the purposes and principles of this Treaty.

CHAPTER THREE

DISARMAMENT AND INTELLIGENCE
Marcus Raskin

The text of this chapter was previously published in the June 8, 1992 issue of The Nation *as an article titled, "Let's Terminate the C.I.A." It is reprinted here with permission for the purpose of integrating into the discussion on disarmament and common security the issue of covert intelligence operations and unconventional warfare. Typically, such discussions focus on nuclear and conventional warfare. Although the analysis below deals specifically with the intelligence agencies of the United States, and is therefore relevant to discussions pertaining to the future role of U.S. intelligence, Raskin's general prescriptions regarding the function of intelligence agencies within the framework of a cooperative security model possess broader significance in this regard.*—ED.

The end of the cold war and the collapse of our chief adversary in that conflict challenges the very existence of the national security state, which has dominated American society for almost a half-century. A pillar of that apparatus is the nation's intelligence community—the Central Intelligence Agency, the National Security Agency, and related agencies. (The U.S. "intelligence community" properly includes the intelligence units in each branch of the armed services, as well as those in the State Department, the Energy Department, the Drug Enforcement Administration, the Justice and Treasury Departments, and the National Imaging Agency.) With an annual secret budget estimated at between $30 billion and $40 billion, these agencies, led by the C.I.A., have been in the forefront of the "secret war" for forty-five years. Aside from rare official inquiries such as the Church committee's investigations in 1975 and periodic exposés in the media, they have operated virtually exempt from public scrutiny. Only when the not uncommon disaster—such as Iran/*contra*—breaks into the headlines do Americans get a glimmer of what is being done in their name by the secret services.

Now that the cold war is over, it is time for a far-reaching public debate on the future role of the intelligence agencies. In my view they should be dismantled or transformed, not merely reorganized. At the confirmation hearings of Robert Gates as Director of Central Intelligence, and in subsequent debates in the Senate, the question of the C.I.A.'s future was raised, but only a few legislators, most notably Senator Daniel Patrick Moynihan, have challenged its cold war premises or questioned its future usefulness. Rather, the approach has been to try to think up new jobs for the C.I.A. The Senate Select Committee on Intelligence entertained such ideas as using the agency to help multinational corporations compete in the global economy or to wage stepped-up antiterrorist campaigns or to collect environmental intelligence.

On February 5, 1992, the chairmen of the Senate and House Intelligence Committees, David Boren and Dave McCurdy, respectively, introduced parallel bills on reorganizing the "intelligence community." But these legislative efforts merely sanctify into law the cold war traditions of U.S. intelligence—covert operations, a threat mentality, a presumption for military intervention and the continuing need for the intelligence community. The "new" intelligence community would be led by a Director of National Intelligence, who would serve as the President's chief adviser on intelligence. Under both bills, the organization and decision making remain under the executive branch. As Senator Ernest Hollings said in committee, the intelligence community should maintain the capacity "to keep policymakers abreast of the great variety of threats the nation faces . . . proliferation of high technology weapons, regional threats, terrorism, drug trafficking, economic and business developments among our trade rivals, and environmental change."

The fact that the senators still think of the intelligence community in terms of the cold war model was obvious in their performance during Gates's confirmation hearings in 1991. During his career, Gates had been involved in a variety of covert activities, cover-ups, and "plausible denials." He claimed that he knew nothing about the Iran/*contra* affair, although he was Deputy Director at the time. As Senator Edward Kennedy, one of the C.I.A.'s few critics, pointed out on the Senate floor, "Mr. Gates's record is one of a cold warrior who skewed intelligence to fit his or his superior's view of the world. He ignored the biggest scandal of the decade, intimidated those who disagreed with his views, and ignored the crumbling of the Soviet Union long after it began."

The C.I.A.'s failure to predict and analyze the likely consequences of a Soviet collapse was an egregious example of its cold war mindset—its fiercely ideological cast, and its belief in the value of stability over change.

Despite Gates's involvement in these agencywide failings and the testimony of other agency officials that he "cooked" intelligence reports to suit the Reagan administration, he was confirmed. The Gates hearings produced evidence that the C.I.A.'s activities were often counterproductive, useless, or even criminal. Yet most senators professed themselves satisfied by Gates's *mea culpas* and accepted as acts of contrition his pledges never to lie to them, to be more open with the public, and to clean up the agency's image.

Last May, seeking to increase congressional control over the C.I.A., Senator John Glenn introduced a bill requiring that top officials of the agency, in addition to the director, be confirmed by the Senate, but this bill, which was tacked onto the Intelligence Authorization Act of 1991, was voted down by the Senate, 59 to 38. Opponents of Glenn's amendment argued that secrecy and czarlike power for the director were still necessary. The Senate's main concerns were about waste and duplication of effort. By April 1992 the Senate intelligence committee returned to its traditional role of covering for the C.I.A., even though the agency lied at least twice to the committee about the transfer of intelligence information to Iraq. After the end of the Gulf War, the C.I.A. told the intelligence committee that the agency had stopped giving intelligence to the Iraqis two years before Iraq's August 1990 invasion of Kuwait. During the Gates nomination hearings the agency changed its tune and said it had ceased cooperating with the Iraqis in early 1990. After the nomination was approved, the C.I.A. said it gave intelligence for another three to four months beyond early 1990. Then further information was released that suggested that the agency continued to give information until August 1990. Senator Boren did not seem bothered by these contradictions.

Reform efforts in Congress have been timid and marginal and will remain dormant until another intelligence scandal surfaces. The opportunity to restructure U.S. intelligence for the post–cold war world has been temporarily lost. Nevertheless, transforming the cold war intelligence apparatus should be a topic of public debate for the rest of this century. The purpose of this analysis of the proper function of intelligence is to contribute to that debate by reconsidering the root assumptions and policy alternatives of national security.

In my view, such a reappraisal will show that the cold war mission of the intelligence community has ended and that it should be dismantled, along with the atmosphere of paranoia and conflict that it fed and propagated at home and abroad. The history of U.S. intelligence over the past forty-five years teaches us what needs to be done if it is to serve democratic ends.

Intelligence and the Cold War

During the cold war years, U.S. intelligence operations were carried out according to a conflict/threat model of international relations. Within that model, American policymakers assumed that the United States is under continuous siege from enemies real or potential, but mostly conjured. It assumed that America's place in the world is primarily achieved through military and covert means. And it assumed that the United States can never be at peace, that it must always be involved in some kind of military or paramilitary activity that it initiates and controls.

American leaders believed that the state required an extensive covert intelligence operation that would assure the nation's superiority in the conflict with its chief enemy, the Soviet Union. Also needed were internal security controls to insure a compliant citizenry. The role of the intelligence community was to perceive the world through the lens of distrust. Institutionalized paranoia was the prescription for the American people, not only against enemies abroad but against their fellow Americans as well.

In addition to the exaggerated fears of Soviet power and intentions, the conflict/threat model presumed a world inhabited by Enemy Others. America's competitive spirit accepted cooperation in military alliances only when the United States was the leading partner. The Soviet Union was portrayed as the archrival, an enduring, pervasive threat that was behind all mischief in the world. To combat it, the United States had to engage in a variety of dirty tricks in the "back alleys" of the world, in Secretary of State Dean Rusk's phrase.

As a recent Pentagon working paper ("Defense Planning Guidance: 1994-1999") indicates, the conflict/threat model is far from dead. Under this Defense Department proposal the United States would preside over a *Pax Americana* and "discourage" advanced industrial nations from "challenging our leadership," as well as deter "potential competitors from even aspiring to a larger or global role." This country, the Pentagon said, "will retain the preeminent responsibility for addressing selectively those wrongs which threaten not only our own interests, but those of our allies or friends, or which could seriously unsettle international relations." Such a policy of world dominance has failure written all over it. As Quincy Wright, a leading international lawyer of the post–World War II era pointed out, "[t]he effort to achieve ideological and political unification by the French Revolution and Napoleon, by the Fascist revolution and Stalin failed and again indicated that co-existence and co-operation among independent nations is the only basis for peace, order, and justice in the world of varied nationalities and ideologies." This reasoning is especially compelling in the aftermath of the collapse of the Soviet Union.

We tend to forget that there is an alternative to the conflict/threat model—the cooperation model. It calls for international cooperation, with nations working through international bodies, adhering to international norms and settling disputes peacefully. The cooperation model gives high priority to finding solutions to the difficult problem of squaring national sovereignty with a code of international human rights, eschewing unilateral intervention, and pursuing a comprehensive disarmament program while establishing an international security arrangement through the Military Staff Committee of the United Nations.

During World War II and immediately after, the cooperation model enjoyed a brief ascendancy, reflecting the U.S.-Soviet alliance, the hopes for the newly formed United Nations, the peoples' yearning for peace. But with the defeat of Henry Wallace's Progressive Party in the 1948 election; the death of two-time G.O.P. presidential candidate Wendell L. Wilkie, whose internationalist ideas dominated the liberal wing of the Republican Party; the rise of McCarthyism; the victory of the Maoists in China; the economic recession of 1949; and the escalation of border skirmishes between the forces of North and South Korea into full-scale war the following year, the conflict/threat model dominated government policy and other institutions as well—cultural, educational, economic.

The bureaucratic rationale for the C.I.A. emerged from fears of officials in the Office of Strategic Services (the wartime precursor to the C.I.A.) that the United States was too dependent on British intelligence, that the Soviet Union was seeking control over Eastern Europe and that adequate information was needed to counterbalance Soviet attempts at expansion. According to Anthony Cave Brown in his book *Wild Bill Donovan: The Last Hero,* a paper, "The Basis for a World-Wide Intelligence Service," was prepared by Lieut. Col. Otto Doering for the chief of the O.S.S., Maj. Gen. William Donovan, in 1944. Doering recommended that such an intelligence service be given, among other things, "access to vouchered and unvouchered funds . . . its own communications systems . . . [responsibility] for all secret activity, including secret intelligence, counterespionage, cryptanalysis, and subversive operations." He hoped that it would grow out of the O.S.S. and would be directly responsible to the President. It would not have any police function.

Donovan revised Doering's paper and sent it to President Roosevelt in November 1944. It presented a comprehensive plan for an intelligence service that "would coordinate, collect and produce finished intelligence, its coordination extended to all government intelligence agencies." Collection would include espionage and counterespionage. The proposed service would also conduct extensive subversive operations abroad and "perform such other functions and duties relating to intelligence" as the President might direct. The production of intelligence would relate to "national planning and security in peace and war," and the new service would have access "to the intelligence production of all other services."

The Donovan paper was leaked to *Chicago Tribune* reporter Walter Trohan, an influential conservative journalist of the period. In a story on the Donovan-Doering plan, he charged that it would create a "super-gestapo agency" to spy on the world. The public and congressional outcry was immediate. Congressional members referred to the proposed agency as the New Deal version of the Soviet O.G.P.U. (the forerunner of the K.G.B.). The leak, which according to Trohan was initiated by Roosevelt through his press secretary, Steve Early, had the effect of sinking Donovan's chances to head the new intelligence agency. Indeed, Congress disbanded the O.S.S., and under the terms of the National Security Act of 1947 set up a new organization to supersede it. The C.I.A. was not much of an improvement over Donovan's model. The major civil liberties safeguard imposed on the C.I.A. was that it was barred from carrying out internal police functions. Soon enough, the C.I.A.—and other intelligence units within the armed forces as well—would compete with the F.B.I. in domestic spying by infiltrating political groups, often for disruptive purposes. The classic cases of such C.I.A. and N.S.A. activities were Operations Chaos and Minaret, which were illegal spying programs against Americans that used warrantless electronic surveillance and human intelligence.

A Game Without Rules

In 1954 a commission appointed by President Eisenhower and chaired by Lieut. Gen. James Doolittle formulated an official rationale to justify intelligence activities already under way. In a key statement, the commission said:

> It is now clear that we are facing an implacable enemy whose avowed objective is world domination by whatever means and at whatever cost. There are no rules in such a game. Hitherto acceptable norms of human conduct do not apply. If the United States is to survive, long-standing American concepts of 'fair play' must be reconsidered. We must . . . learn to subvert, sabotage and destroy our enemies by more clever, more sophisticated and more effective methods than those used against us.
>
> It also concluded that "[a]nother important requirement is an aggressive covert psychological, political and paramilitary organization more effective, more unique and, if necessary, more ruthless than that employed by the enemy. No one should be permitted to stand in the way of the prompt, efficient and secure accomplishment of this mission."

Spying was indeed a dirty business. The operations of the C.I.A. and other agencies were often immoral, unconstitutional, and criminal. Such activities would have made the public uneasy, so they had to be shrouded by the arts of secrecy and plausible denial. Since the C.I.A. often operated as the president's private army, the executive branch became a kind of front for illegal covert actions. The president gave them a patina of legitimacy, thereby turning the office into a switching point between criminal and lawful activities. Sometimes, of course, presidents or their subordinates were caught flat-footed participating in criminal activities, as when Howard Hunt, a former C.I.A. agent working for the White House, used the agency to help him break into the office of Daniel Ellsberg's psychiatrist.

Secrecy also served to shield the intelligence establishment (and its hefty budgets) from congressional and media scrutiny. It insulated the C.I.A. from public examination that might have prevented it from launching disastrous operations like the Bay of Pigs invasion or Operation Phoenix in Vietnam, in which some 20,000 innocent people and suspected Vietcong supporters were murdered. Without outside criticism of its past mistakes, the C.I.A. was doomed to repeat them.

And so for decades it conducted interventions worldwide, subverting governments, arming insurgencies, spreading black propaganda. Often these actions produced harmful consequences. The "victorious coup" in Iran that expelled Mossadegh brought back the Shah, whose misrule paved the way for the Ayatollah Khomeini. The 1954 coup that overthrew Guatemala's democratically elected government produced decades of cruel dictatorship. The glorious putsch that expelled Sukarno in Indonesia brought in its wake the murder or imprisonment of hundreds of thousands of Indonesians. Back in Washington, the exaggerations of the intelligence community fed and sustained the arms race.

Scholars and Spies

The benign view of itself the C.I.A. projected—as a mere gatherer and dispenser of information to the president from its "campus" at Langley, Virginia, where strolled professorial, pipe-smoking types—was gradually eroded by belated revelations that some of these men had conducted experiments on unwilling subjects with mind-altering drugs, had used germ warfare agents against poor nations, and had planned and executed coups.

As the Gates hearings showed, the C.I.A.'s "scholars and spies" were hardly dedicated to independent inquiry. Often their analyses were slanted to pander to the desires of the policymakers and the predilections of the national security curia. To advance their careers, junior analysts skewed their reports to harmonize with what the "hierarchic other," or superiors in the organization, wanted.

Secrecy invariably assumes a priesthood dealing in fixed truths and essences. It is the antithesis of the spirit of free inquiry exemplified in the teachings of pragmatism, the leading twentieth-century school of social thought. As John Dewey pointed out, "intelligence," in its full meaning as a powerful instrument of social action, can work only as a *public* activity, in settings where judgments and conclusions can be cross-examined and verified through open inquiry and further discourse. "The one fact," he wrote in *Ethics,* "which is most certain is that throughout social life as a whole the older idea and practice which made knowledge a monopolistic possession still persists in a way which prevents the realization and even the fair trial of the democratic ideal. . . . The problem of bringing about an effective socialization of intelligence is probably the greatest problem of democracy today."

A secret bureaucracy, a policy of secrets within secrets, disclosed only to those with "a need to know," by its very nature engenders paranoia, institutional ignorance and control by a handful of executives, especially in the context of the conflict/threat mindset. The career of James Jesus Angleton, the poet manque and former head of C.I.A. counterintelligence, exemplified this tendency toward paranoia at the highest levels. Angleton apparently concluded that William Colby, a former Director of Central Intelligence and the head of Operation Phoenix, was a mole for the Soviet Union. Angleton's malign suspicions, fed by a Soviet defector, rocked the agency for more than a decade.

Angleton's case is perhaps extreme. In the closed society of the intelligence community, what the analyst concludes may be distorted by institutional pressures and a deep-seated policy that goes unquestioned but that distorts analysts' structuring of the data. In an intelligence agency millions of pieces of data are processed daily. As in any scientific inquiry, this flux must be arranged into some order, and the task of the analyst is to make an existential judgment of what he or she believes to be true or authentic. But what is found to be authentic in the closed society of intelligence may derive from a desire or a vested interest simply to please the boss. Undeniably, these factors are at work on other, nonsecret agencies of government. But there is an important difference: "Open" governmental agencies operate with some degree of accountability to Congress, the courts and, through the media, the public.

Covert Wars

But intelligence collection and analysis sometimes seemed the least of the C.I.A.'s purposes. The agency has generally been more interested in carrying out direct paramilitary interventions with the sanction of Congress or the president or, sometimes, on its own motion. In September 1970 President Nixon ordered C.I.A. Director Richard Helms to take measures to make the Chilean economy "scream" in order to destabilize the government of socialist President Salvador Allende. Assassination attempts were made against unwanted foreign leaders, usually leftists like Patrice Lumumba in the Congo. Cuba's Fidel Castro has been a favorite *bete noire* since the Eisenhower administration. But rightists were not immune. In the Dominican Republic, Rafael Trujillo, a right-wing dictator who had lost the confidence of Washington, was assassinated in 1961. C.I.A. "assets" who became leaders of their country and showed some independence, like Panama's Manuel Noriega, were cut down to size. Under the Reagan administration C.I.A.-backed surrogates, or "freedom fighters," waged wars in Nicaragua, El Salvador, Afghanistan, Angola, Cambodia, and Chad. Covert support to diverse elements in Eastern Europe was stepped up.

C.I.A. Director William Casey served as the field marshal of a worldwide system of covert wars. No area of the world was immune from intervention by the C.I.A., N.S.A. and other agencies. All of these escapades flowed from what Frank Wisner, former Deputy Director of the C.I.A., once called "the mighty Wurlitzer"—the ten aspects of intelligence work. Each activity is inextricably linked to the others; like an onion, peel away one layer and you reach another, more dangerous level. The ten are:

1. The gathering of information by overt or covert means (if the information is gathered by covert means, then as likely as not, another nation's laws are violated).

2. Evaluating, analyzing, and storing information; finding assets (covert sources) and establishing proprietaries (dummy companies) to undertake specific tasks.

3. Advising and disseminating information that is often false and self-deceiving; getting U.S. government consumers to use the information, developing a market for it and fashioning information and facts that are custom-made for particular clients in the government. The market may want untruthful information or lies.

4. Persuading government consumers to use information they may not ordinarily be interested in (an organization dependent on the whim of a president must provide him with what he wants, but he may bore easily, and so irrelevant or tabloidlike information has to be generated to keep presidential interest).

5. Organizing more covert activities to obtain information, verify conclusions, and answer new requests of policymakers. This is accomplished by expanding the asset and informant network within the United States and abroad; reading intelligence material from other nations and other agencies within the government or from corporations; finding, then relying on, more intelligence material that is gathered secretly or through technical means; bribing and paying assets who are members of other governments.

6. Organizing clandestine activities to obtain classified information of other nations as well as undertaking disinformation campaigns in which material is manufactured to promote either the position of the C.I.A., the official policies of the United States, the agendas of specific groups within the intelligence community, or policies that are contrary to those stated to Congress or that violate American law (it should be noted that such disinformation has often found itself blown back into the United States, where it was used to whip up political support for positions that had no factual predicate).

7. Organizing black operations of a complex nature such as economic and political destabilization, mining harbors, funding third-party nations to do the bidding of the United States (as in the case of Israel) as well as receiving and organizing proxy funds.

8. Employing scientific and technological means to undercut the development or abort or inhibit the activities of an adversary nation; developing technical intelligence capacity, cryptography and topographic analysis through satellites.

9. Recruiting local armies and guerrilla groups and developing and guiding them so they can be used for the national objectives of the United States. Covertly sponsoring labor unions, women's groups, and paying for crowds and demonstrators.

10. Using force—assassination teams when necessary—to assert the considered (or ill-considered) policy. Fighting small wars that are kept out of the U.S. media. Shielding the president by offering plausible denial and cover for illegal and criminal actions he ordered.

These activities form the foundation stones of the intelligence community. The entire project of this community helped to make the government of the United States into an Orwellian nightmare, in which "intelligence" became synonymous with massive self-deception and treachery. Force and fraud had found a home base in the intelligence community and in the cold war conception of intelligence.

Cooperative Security and Intelligence

The United States is now at a turning point: It must decide what sort of nation it wants to be. The future role of the intelligence community will have a direct bearing on the character of our nation, for the intelligence community helps determine the policymakers' perception of the world. It can sustain myths, generate and authenticate "threats," and give the color of rationality to force and fraud.

The struggles now smoldering in Eastern Europe and the former Soviet Union, the clan animosities raging from Angola to Croatia, the endemic tensions in the Middle East and elsewhere in the world provide plenty of potential stages for future intelligence actions should we decide to continue playing the dirty game of back-alley wars.

But there is an alternative: adopting the cooperation model. This would mean dismantling the present intelligence community, abandoning those functions that served the cold war state and reassigning to other agencies the functions that can be integrated into the cooperation model of international relations. In this scheme, intelligence analysis would be used as a communications bridge among nations rather than as a tool for power and control.

The cooperation model would be based on the premise that the problems of our world at the close of the twentieth century cannot be resolved by a single nation, the United States, pursuing its own ends. The environment, immigration, disarmament, economic justice and health, as well as the need for mediating regional and international disputes are matters of world concern requiring the public exchange of ideas and information among a wide array of very different national cultures. A shift away from the conflict/threat paradigm, which means demilitarization and the shifting of budget expenditures away from militarized national security policies, would free badly needed resources to deal with this country's pressing domestic problems.

The United States is in the best position to lead the shift to the cooperation model because its military security problems can be dealt with through a worldwide general disarmament process in tandem with the strengthening of U.N. peacekeeping functions.

Under the cooperation model, intelligence would of course cease to be a clandestine enterprise. Instead it would operate as an international social project, in tandem with a new foreign policy agenda dedicated to environmental protection, scientific understanding, improved communications and information dispersal, worldwide economic development, health improvement, and military disarmament.

Steps to an Open Society

The following changes should be made in the U.S. intelligence community to enable it to serve the United States as a nation willing to act within the cooperation model of international politics. Although some of the proposed changes are relevant only to the U.S. intelligence community, many of these proposals possess general relevance to a cooperative security model.

Step One. There should be a comprehensive revision of the National Security Act of 1947 to insure that the United States pursues policies of cooperation with the United Nations and respect for international law and human rights. The act's purpose, to "provide a comprehensive program for the future security of the United States," cannot be achieved under its current philosophy of militarization of governmental thought, command and organization, and of the employment of resources for war and conflict. The language of a revised National Security Act would emphasize global disarmament, stimulation of international communication, reinvestment in the U.S. infrastructure, preservation of the environment, protection of human rights, and cooperation on common problems among nations in the post–cold war world. Intelligence activities would be harnessed to achieving those ends.

Step Two. There should be a review of all laws and executive orders that give the intelligence community special status. The most relevant examples are laws that exempt various agencies from systematic review of their operations, from the federal pay scale and from federal labor-management relations statutes. We should also abolish the law exempting the C.I.A. retirement system from public scrutiny and the C.I.A., N.S.A., Defense Intelligence Agency and certain other intelligence units from public financial disclosure requirements.

Several other cold war laws should be repealed or revised, including those making intelligence agencies only vaguely accountable for how they spend their money. There are also statutes that protect members of the C.I.A. from false identification laws, computer fraud statutes, as well as those that allow interference with satellite transmissions. These laws violate the elementary principles of openness, democracy, and cooperation that are necessary to international cooperation in the post–cold war world.

Step Three. The C.I.A.'s analytic functions should be transferred to noncovert agencies of government. This would affect some nongovernmental sectors of society as well—the universities, international corporations, labor unions, and media that have maintained a symbiotic relationship with the national security state, including with the intelligence agencies, since World War II.

The idea that knowledge and information know no boundaries, which dominated the scientific community before World War II, should be revived. The data-collection and analysis functions of the C.I.A. and N.S.A. should be internationalized much in the manner that medical information is now exchanged internationally and publicly. The information could be made available as part of an international information agency that would establish regional centers. The United States, with the assent of the U.N. Security Council and General Assembly, could form a worldwide consortium of intelligence agencies, served by a worldwide community of scholars and analysts whose researches would be made public and distributed widely through regional centers. It would be understood that this consortium would operate under the United Nations. Just as no nation can afford not to trade internationally, so no nation or society can afford not to share information for the common good.

The specific areas on which this consortium would concentrate are scientific and data gathering and dissemination; economic justice reporting; conflict resolution; environmental enhancement; the state of human rights; and the state of international agreements, especially in the disarmament area.

Step Four. The paramilitary functions that the C.I.A. performed during the cold war should be placed under the control of the uniformed military services, where they would be subjected to public scrutiny and civilian control. The War Powers Act and Article I, Section 8 of the Constitution, which gives Congress the power to declare war, govern the president's use of military power except when the United States is attacked. C.I.A. covert actions under the military would be publicly accountable. To underscore this point, the laws on mercenaries should be amended so that they apply directly to government officials or their agents. These sections of the law now make it a crime for individuals to conspire on U.S. soil to destroy the property of or to organize a military expedition against a nation with which the United States is at peace. But penalties are relatively light, no more than three years in prison and/or a $5,000 fine. They should be substantially increased. Throughout the cold war, covert activities, many of them unauthorized, took place under the color of bureaucratic legality. In the future, rogue operators or those who otherwise transgress legal authority would be subject to criminal prosecution.

In other words, military interventions, economic destabilization, and other covert actions would be deemed criminal offenses. A president who sought to avoid constitutional constraints by running a secret war or intervention would face impeachment.

Step Five. The Secretary of State should set forth a needs and requirements reports to Congress in order to improve the political reporting of the State Department. The secretary will make clear that the department will absorb analysts from the C.I.A., but that it will not countenance being used as a cover for covert and clandestine activities.

Step Six. A Protection of Records Act should be crafted to insure that no records of the C.I.A. or other intelligence agencies are destroyed. In this way a true account of the history of the cold war period could be written. These records should be made public as quickly as possible after being transferred to the Archivist of the United States. Substantial penalties should apply to those government officials who attempt to forge or rewrite the record.

Step Seven. Except for that part of the National Security Agency that would be given over to the Arms Control and Disarmament Agency and, for specific and narrowly defined purposes, the Defense Department, the N.S.A. would become an international public library under the control of the Librarian of Congress and secondarily the Archivist of the United States.

Any residual activities of the N.S.A. should be subjected to rigorous public scrutiny by Congress in order to assure that its information be made publicly available, and to assure that its various activities are in fact constitutionally sanctioned.

The use of technical intelligence to assure compliance with arms control and disarmament agreements should be strengthened. The N.S.A. could link up with similar agencies throughout the world for the specific purpose of observing military maneuvers and the production and shipment of arms, as well as adhering to the disarmament process. All activities having to do with monitoring arms control and disarmament arrangements could be supervised by the Arms Control and Disarmament Agency and could be publicly conducted, with the N.S.A. serving as the technical arm.

Step Eight. Throughout the cold war, security procedures and surveillance of government officials have been used as an *in terrorem* policy to protect secrets and enforce loyalty. These secrets, as often as not, have reflected two types of material. The first broad category is related to technical scientific matters and military plans. The second is related to operations that were in violation of American law or the law of other nations and international law. Security procedures that in fact have been thinly veiled cover-up schemes (for example, Iran/*contra*) should now be forbidden by executive order.

Matters that pertain to the defense of the United States would continue to be secret. Such secrecy is warranted so long as classification is carried out by the Defense Department as part of its constitutional mandate and pertains to defensive measures permitted by the U.N. Charter, international law, and the laws of the United States. However, the entire system of classifying documents would require comprehensive revision so that it would conform to the revised National Security Act described in Step One.

Step Nine. Under Article I, Section 5 of the Constitution, "each House may determine the rules of proceedings" and "each House shall keep a journal of its proceedings, and from time to time publish the same, excepting such parts as may in their judgment require secrecy." This section would appear to give ample support to the idea of secret hearings (executive session). However, during the cold war this rule of prudence of the Constitution was severely abused. Secrecy was used as a way of co-opting various members of Congress and committees into intelligence activities that would ordinarily be subject to legal challenge, criticism, and debate.

Conclusion

The end of the cold war is the right time to restore a rule that is clearly contemplated by the Constitution, namely, that secrecy in government is the exception and not the normal way of doing business. Congress itself should now revise its own organizational structure on national security matters. It should re-examine its own assumptions regarding secrecy and the harm caused by its failure to be an independent and disinterested guardian over the intelligence agencies. House Rule XLVIII, which governs the House Permanent Select Committee on Intelligence, begins from the assumption of secrecy and nondisclosure of information. Senate Resolution 400, which established its Select Committee on Intelligence, also assumes that its work is primarily secret. The irony is that concern about leaks by congressional members is greater than concern about the actual practices of the intelligence agencies.

The United States is a protean organism; it can change its shape and purpose. And it can assist in giving birth to a cooperative world civilization that recognizes the importance of cultures and nations outside Europe. If American leaders attempt to control a messy, recalcitrant reality through military and covert means, if the nation does not take stock of itself and initiate its own internal reconstruction, then we will indeed live a nightmare of decline and continuous war, with the covert agencies leading the way. We will mistake paranoia for intelligence, and American leaders will be seeking new Enemy Others to justify the national security state. Without substantial changes in attitudes and direction, the intelligence community will be a willing accomplice, supplying or inventing new threats to an insecure leadership and nation. This year the threat could be the Japanese and next year the Germans, or perhaps it is Iraq or Iran or Libya, or Croatians, North Koreans, African-Americans, or immigrants, that justify covert operations.

It is time for the executive and Congress to come in from the cold. It is time for knowledge workers inside and outside governments to work together and fashion a world cooperation model that could help humanity transcend the horrible follies of the twentieth century.

CHAPTER FOUR

DISARMAMENT AND INTERNATIONAL LAW
Howard Friel

In chapter 2, Marcus Raskin presents a comprehensive disarmament treaty that seeks the worldwide abolition of nuclear weapons and offense-capable conventional forces from the military arsenals of each nation (see Raskin Treaty article 2[2]). The Raskin Treaty specifies that, upon full implementation of the disarmament regime, each state may retain "nonnuclear, nonoffensive defenses to be configured as border guard, coast guard, and air defense forces" and that "[t]he maximum capabilities of these forces shall not constitute a capability or threat to attack or invade the territorial borders of any other state" (see article 2[3]).

The treaty further states that, "[f]or the purposes of maintaining a collective self-defense and peacekeeping force" under the command of the United Nations, a "separation of capabilities" formula should be applied to the configuration of these U.N. forces (see article 2[6]). Implementation of the separation of capabilities principle "would require that the retained military capabilities" of the United Nations be configured in such a way "that no single country or region would retain a self-possessed interventionist capability" (see Raskin Treaty Commentary, article 2[6]).

Taken together, these treaty provisions constitute a disarmament model possessing two essential aspects—abolition of the instruments of aggressive war, and an alternative security program based upon the military doctrines of nonoffensive defense and collective security—that arguably possess corresponding foundations in fundamental principles of international law. This integration of disarmament goals and international law principles constitutes a significant conceptual advance toward an authoritative model for world peace, given the global legitimacy of international law and the Raskin Treaty's application of these universal and nondiscriminatory principles to a general disarmament regime. Thus, what the design of the Raskin Treaty proposes is consideration of the following proposition: Can a world-order model be developed that possesses the legitimacy of international law, that can function as the "negotiating mandate" for a comprehensive disarmament regime, and that would satisfy the desire and obligation of each state to guarantee its own territorial security? These are the questions that will be examined in this chapter.

Disarmament, Nuclear Weapons, and International Law

Although it is generally recognized that the customary laws of war apply to weapons of mass destruction—a recognition that has led to express prohibitions of use, manufacture, and stockpiling of biological and chemical weapons and poisonous gases[1]—some states possessing nuclear weapons have argued that these same laws of war do not apply as such to nuclear weapons, and that since an international treaty does not exist that expressly prohibits the use, manufacture, or possession of nuclear weapons, nuclear weapons are not likewise prohibited.[2]

The long-standing, declared position of the United States in this regard is stated as follows:

> The use of explosive "atomic weapons," whether by air, sea or land forces, cannot as such be regarded as violative of international law in the absence of any customary rule of international law or international convention restricting their employment.[3]

This statement has been interpreted to mean that nuclear weapons are legal weapons under international law, and though subject to the regulations of the customary laws of war as is the use of any legal weapon, these laws of war do not outlaw nuclear weapons in a wide range of possible uses and deployments.

Although this position may represent the declared policy of the United States with regard to nuclear weapons and international law, involving as it does an implied recognition that customary international law imposes in principle some limitations on the use of nuclear weapons, the operational policy of the United States with regard to nuclear weapons, involving as it does full-blown deployment and targeting of a massive strategic and tactical nuclear weapons arsenal, clearly signifies nonrecognition of even minimal limitations on the use of nuclear weapons imposed by the customary laws of war.[4]

These customary laws of war prohibit the use of weapons of mass destruction that (a) are indiscriminate in their use between civilian and noncivilian targets; (b) have effects that are disproportionate to legitimate military objectives; (c) violate the neutral jurisdiction of nonbelligerent states; (d) effect reprisals that are disproportionate to the antecedent provocation; (e) cause widespread, long-term, and severe damage to the environment; and (f) use asphyxiating, poisonous or other gases, and all analogous liquids, materials and devices.[5] Since the use of even a fraction of the U.S. nuclear arsenal in almost all instances would result in injury as described in these principles of customary international law, it is clear that the United States recognizes no customary international law restraints upon the use of nuclear weapons.

In recent years, many highly qualified analysts have challenged the policies manifesting the view that nuclear weapons are legal weapons under international law, and that no international convention or customary rule of international law prohibits their use and deployment.[6] Writing in 1987 as a professor of law at Monash University in Australia, Christopher G. Weeramantry, who has since been elected to serve as one of the fifteen judges at the International Court of Justice, argued that the principles of international law outlaw nuclear weapons:

> Among the sources of international law enumerated by Article 38 of the Charter of the International Court of Justice are international custom, the general principles of law recognized by civilized nations, judicial decisions, and the opinions of outstanding jurists, all of which strongly establish the illegality of nuclear weaponry.
>
> The absence of a specific treaty banning the use or manufacture of nuclear weapons means that only one of the sources of international law is absent. . . . It is sometimes argued that nuclear weapons do not come within the scope of laws of war which were formulated before their invention. This is a spurious argument. . . . What is important is the principle underlying the rule. Specific applications of the general principle occur in the light of events and circumstances that only arise later. Nearly every piece of legislation and nearly every Constitution (that of the U.S. is the best example) must be applied to situations that were not envisaged when they were formulated. These sources of law would only be inoperative if they had no general principle which would cover the new situation. In the case of nuclear weapons, those general principles do exist.[7]

Contrasting the nuclear weapons policies of the states possessing nuclear weapons with the obligations inherent in the principles of customary international law described above and referred to by Judge Weeramantry, the four-person London Nuclear Warfare Tribunal—which was chaired by Sean MacBride, a Nobel Peace Prize recipient, and which also included Professor Richard Falk of Princeton University—argued that "[u]pon the evidence, the use of nuclear weapons cannot distinguish between combatants and non-combatants, does not represent a proportionate use of force, cannot be selective or discriminating, and violates the rights of neutral nations. In short, the use of nuclear weapons is unlawful."[8]

The conclusion of the London Tribunal is consistent with the majority view in the U.N. General Assembly that the use of nuclear weapons is illegal under international law. In a 1961 resolution titled "Declaration on the Prohibition of the Use of Nuclear and Thermonuclear Weapons," the General Assembly declared that

> [t]he use of nuclear and thermonuclear weapons is contrary to the spirit, letter and aims of the United Nations and, as such, a direct violation of the Charter of the United Nations. . . . Any State using nuclear and thermonuclear weapons is to be considered as violating the Charter of the United Nations, as acting contrary to the laws of humanity and as committing a crime against mankind and civilizations.[9]

The General Assembly subsequently declared in resolutions in 1978, 1980, 1981, 1990, and 1991 that the use of nuclear weapons would violate the U.N. Charter and the customary laws of war.[10] (These resolutions coincide with the General Assembly's authority under U.N. Charter article 11 to consider the principles governing disarmament and the regulation of armaments and to make recommendations with respect to such principles, as well as its authority under article 10 to make recommendations with respect to the development of international law.[11])

In May 1992 three prestigious organizations declared their view that the use and threat of use of nuclear weapons is illegal under international law: the International Association of Lawyers Against Nuclear Arms (IALANA), with thousands of members in over twenty affiliated organizations around the world; the International Peace Bureau (IPB), which received the Nobel Peace Prize in 1910; and the International Physicians for the Prevention of Nuclear War (IPPNW), a membership organization of 200,000 physicians worldwide that received the Nobel Peace Prize in 1985. In the declaration these groups announced their intention to petition a U.N.-affiliated agency to seek an advisory opinion from the International Court of Justice on the legality of the use and threat of use of nuclear weapons.[12] And in 1986 the IPB's Appeal by Lawyers Against Nuclear War, endorsed by thousands of lawyers around the world, stated that "the use, for whatever reason, of a nuclear weapon would constitute (a) a violation of international law, (b) a violation of human rights, and (c) a crime against humanity."[13]

Several highly qualified individual jurists affiliated with the Lawyers Committee on Nuclear Policy have also argued that the use of nuclear weapons is illegal under international law. Professor Burns H. Weston of The University of Iowa College of Law, and a member of the Board of Directors of the Lawyers Committee, has argued that "[i]t is essential to the evolution of a peaceful and just global polity that the strategic planners and apologists among the nuclear-weapons States—especially the defense policy-makers, the military operators, the laboratories of military research and development, the arms controllers, the politicians, even the jurists—come to see the incompatibility of nuclear weapons with the core precepts of international law."[14] Professor Francis A. Boyle of the University of Illinois College of Law, also a member of the Board of Directors of the Lawyers Committee, has argued that "[t]he use of nuclear weapons in combat is absolutely prohibited under all circumstances by both conventional and customary international law, for example, [by] the Nuremberg Principles, the Hague Regulations of 1907, the International Convention on the Prevention and Punishment of the Crime of Genocide of 1948, the Four Geneva Conventions of 1949 and their Additional Protocol I of 1977, etc."[15] And the Lawyers Committee on Nuclear Policy, as an expression of the organization's views, has stated that "[a]lmost every use to which nuclear weapons might be put, most notably the standard strategic and theater-level options . . . violates one or more of the laws of war."[16]

Once one interprets international law as prohibiting the use of nuclear weapons, it is possible to establish the illegality of the threat of use of nuclear weapons—the threat of use being the fundamental component of the nuclear deterrence doctrine. In a legal memorandum representing the position of the three international organizations mentioned above—IALANA, IPB, and IPPNW—Nicholas Grief, a professor of law at the University of Exeter in England, spoke to the illegality of the threat of use of nuclear weapons as follows:

> If the use of nuclear weapons is contrary to international law, then logically any threat of such use must also be illegal. The symbiotic relationship between the illegality of use and threat is reflected in the cardinal rule of international law, Article 2(4) of the U.N. Charter, which prohibits "the threat or use of force" by a state in the conduct of its international relations. Under this most fundamental rule, when use is prohibited, the threat of such use is also prohibited. Therefore, once one establishes the illegality of the use of nuclear weapons under the U.N. Charter, one may establish the illegality of the threat of use of nuclear weapons under the U.N. Charter. Since Article 2(4) prohibits the threat or use of force "against the territorial integrity or political independence of any State, or in any other manner inconsistent with the Purposes of the United Nations," and since the use of nuclear weapons would clearly be "inconsistent with the Purposes of the United Nations," and, therefore, illegal under the U.N. Charter, it follows from Article 2(4) that the threat of use of nuclear weapons would constitute a violation of the U.N. Charter as well.[17]

The members of the London Nuclear Warfare Tribunal have argued similarly: "It is apparent, given the assumption that the use of nuclear weapons is unlawful, that the planning and preparation [to use nuclear weapons] in breach of such treaties is also unlawful."[18]

In their extensive opinion on nuclear weapons and international law, the members of the London Tribunal argued that the possession of nuclear weapons, war plans to use nuclear weapons, and the threat of use of nuclear weapons expressed in such plans are illegal under international law:

> All legal systems endeavor not merely to punish crime but also to prevent it. Obviously, it is a rather ineffectual system which can only deal with crime once its effects have been felt. Accordingly, in all criminal jurisdictions intentional preparation to commit crime is itself a crime. . . . The laws of war are no exception. Thus, Article 6(a) of the Nuremberg Charter defines the term "crime against peace" as "the planning, preparation, initiation or waging of a war of aggression, or a war in violation of international treaties or agreements or assurances or participation in a common plan or conspiracy for the accomplishment of any of the foregoing." . . . The point is a simple one: If the consequences of the intended actions are themselves illegal, then preparation to inflict such conflict is also illegal. Whatever their disclaimers as to the use of nuclear weapons, the nuclear weapons states are expressly and by implication planning and preparing unlawful actions—the infliction of indiscriminate destruction. The development, deployment, and targeting of nuclear weapons have no other rational interpretation.[19]

The Tribunal concluded that "the possession of nuclear weapons and planning of a nuclear war are in breach of Article 6(a) of the Nuremberg Charter" and that "an individual or organization agreeing to be part of a system which leads to the use of nuclear weapons is also in breach of the relevant Nuremberg Principles."[20]

Finally, the leaders of states possessing nuclear weapons also argue that the deployment and use of nuclear weapons for deterrence purposes is justified by the self-defense provisions of U.N. Charter article 51.[21] The members of the London Nuclear Warfare Tribunal responded to the self-defense argument as it relates to nuclear weapons:

> It is no answer under the [U.N.] Charter, nor under any other legal system that we know of, to say that one is merely preparing to act in self-defense where the consequences of such actions are so wholly unreasonable. It is dishonest and perverse to suggest that the unlimited and indiscriminate damage which would result from a nuclear exchange can ever be described as reasonable self-defense. The proposition offends against the entire concept of reason.[22]

Judge Weeramantry has also responded to the self-defense justification of the nuclear weapons states:

> From the standpoint of international law, such retaliatory or revengeful slaughter of enemy populations would not be covered by the justification of self-defense. Indeed, it is a concept totally different from self-defence in content, quality and objective. . . . In short, the self-defence argument

is a self-serving justification masking the inherent illegality of nuclear weapons.[23]

To summarize, because the legal evidence strongly suggests that fundamental principles of international law do apply to nuclear weapons; because the weight of legal precedent is to prohibit the development, production, stockpiling, and use of weapons of mass destruction; because there are no international law principles justifying the use or threat of use of weapons of mass destruction; and because, as the London Tribunal has stated, "it is difficult to identify any real value system that justifies their use,"[24] it is clear that the use of nuclear weapons, as well as the policies of the states that possess, deploy, target, and threaten the use of nuclear weapons, are illegal under international law.

Given the illegality of nuclear weapons under international law, a disarmament regime based upon international law criteria, such as the Raskin Treaty regime, would require the elimination of nuclear weapons from each nation's arsenal.

Disarmament, Nonoffensive Defense, and International Law

To be effective, a global agreement on disarmament and common security must function not only as an agreement on the quantitative reduction of armaments but also as an accord on standards of international conduct. In fact, without prior consensus on what is both permissible and prohibited with regard to the behavior of states in the conduct of their international relations, it is doubtful that the community of states would agree to disarm to levels that would mandate, in a *de facto* sense, universal standards of behavior. Likewise, a consensus on conduct and behavior would help determine the final configuration of permissible military allotments, since no state would be permitted to retain the military capability to carry out prohibited behavior. Thus, fundamental to the design of a disarmament and common security regime is the establishment of a code of peaceful conduct that would prescribe permissible standards of international conduct as well as help determine the disarmament blueprint. In fact, a legally binding code of peaceful conduct among nations already exists: it is embodied in the rules and principles of international law, including the U.N. Charter, the most authoritative source of international law.

A Code of Peaceful Conduct

A good-faith interpretation of the U.N. Charter would identify what must be seen as the cardinal rule of any code of peaceful conduct among nations: a prohibition on the use and threat of use of force by states in the conduct of their international relations, except in response to an armed attack upon territorial borders, or as part of a U.N.-sponsored collective defense or peacekeeping action.[25]

A similar interpretation of the Nuremberg Principles would lead to the second rule in the code of peaceful conduct: a prohibition on planning or preparing for aggressive war, including a prohibition on the manufacture, possession, testing, and deployment of armaments that reflect an intention to wage aggressive war; that is, a use of force that is not a response to an armed attack on territorial borders, that is not part of a U.N.-sponsored action, or that otherwise violates international law or agreements.[26]

The third rule in the code of peaceful conduct would entail a commitment to a disarmament regime based upon the "nonoffensive defense" military doctrine that is derivative of the first two rules. Nonoffensive defense, as developed in this chapter, is a military doctrine whereby the nations of the world would eliminate the capability to wage aggressive war while retaining only the capability to defend their territorial borders and participate in U.N.-sponsored military actions.[27]

A comprehensive disarmament regime based upon this code of international conduct, if implemented, would satisfy each country's international law requirements, guarantee the territorial integrity of each state, and reduce global military expenditures to levels necessary only for the maintenance of territorial defense and U.N.-sponsored forces. Thus, the nonoffensive defense doctrine that is derived from this code of conduct and used as a disarmament criterion provides the global legitimacy of international law, the military legitimacy of territorial defense, and the moral legitimacy of efforts leading to the abolition of aggressive war and its instruments.

An analysis of the international law foundation of a disarmament regime grounded in the nonoffensive defense doctrine is presented below.

Nonoffensive Defense and International Law

U.N. Charter article 2(4) prohibits the use or threat of use of force by a state in the conduct of its international relations. The article states:

> All Members shall refrain in their international relations from the threat or use of force against the territorial integrity or political independence of any state, or in any other manner inconsistent with the Purposes of the United Nations.

This rule is widely regarded as the cardinal rule of international law, the world-ordering legal principle of the post–World War II era.

However, U.N. Charter article 51 provides an exception to this basic rule by permitting a state to resort to force in self-defense in response to an armed attack upon its borders:

Nothing in the present Charter shall impair the inherent right of individual or collective self-defense if an armed attack occurs against a Member of the United Nations, until the Security Council has taken the measures necessary to maintain international peace and security. Measures taken by Members in the exercise of this right of self-defense shall be immediately reported to the Security Council and shall not in any way affect the authority and responsibility of the Security Council under the present Charter to take at any time such action as it deems necessary in order to maintain or restore international peace and security.

Since World War II and the founding of the United Nations, several states have broadly interpreted their right to resort to force in self-defense, often claiming wide latitude to use military force beyond its borders. The Soviet Union, for example, justified its invasions of Hungary (1956), Czechoslovakia (1968), and Afghanistan (1979) by citing its right to self-defense against alleged Western subversion of its satellite states.[28] The United States has also justified its military interventions in Vietnam in the 1960s, and in Grenada, Libya, Nicaragua, and Panama in the 1980s, by citing its legal right to self-defense under the U.N. Charter.[29]

In response to the distortion and misapplication of the right to self-defense under international law, many international law scholars and concerned citizens throughout the world have challenged the integrity of the intervention-justifying interpretation of the right to self-defense. These efforts perhaps culminated in December 1988 when former Soviet President Mikhail Gorbachev implicitly renounced at the United Nations his own country's policy of resorting to force outside its own borders, and appealed to the world community to reaffirm the prohibition of the use of force as an instrument of international affairs.[30]

One product of the Gorbachev-sponsored change in Soviet policy was a series of disarmament proposals that expressed in terms of military hardware the changes that had occurred in the policy software.[31] Even after the breakup of the Soviet Union, the commitment to a Russian foreign policy grounded in international law is still apparent. As recently as November 19, 1992, Russian President Boris Yeltsin, while on an official state visit to South Korea, announced the Russian intention to disarm its conventional military forces to levels sufficient only for the defense of Russian borders.[32]

The response from the West to these Soviet and Russian initiatives has been slow. The kind of analysis and open debate that developed in the Soviet Union throughout the last half of the 1980s and that brought about a fundamental change in Soviet policy and commitment to international law has not occurred, for example, in the United States. Such a debate, if it is to take place, must include a glasnost-style willingness to reexamine the long-standing U.S. policy of military intervention as well as the official interpretation of international law that has been used repeatedly to justify this policy.

As both a global superpower and the Western nation with the highest incidence of intervention in the post–World War II period, a reexamination of U.S. foreign policy principles would go a long way toward convincing its allies and adversaries that for the purposes of a worldwide movement toward disarmament, common security, and adherence to international law, the prerequisite ideological and policy changes are not beyond the reach of any nation.

Vietnam and International Law

Twenty-five years ago, an important debate regarding fundamental principles of international law took place when the Lawyers Committee on American Policy Toward Vietnam—the forerunner group to the Lawyers Committee on Nuclear Policy chaired by Richard Falk—published an interpretation of the right to self-defense under international law that challenged the official interpretation of that right by President Lyndon Johnson's State Department.[33] The Johnson administration had justified its military escalation in Vietnam in 1965 on the claim of a U.S. right to self-defense under international law. At the time, several points of international law were in dispute between the State Department and the Lawyers Committee on Vietnam. These points are itemized below. As the members of the Lawyers Committee commented at that time: "This examination is not concerned with fine points of legalism. At stake are the fundamental principles of world order."[34] Indeed, once one grasps the interpretation of international law advanced by the Lawyers Committee during the Vietnam War, it is possible to recognize the relevance of the Lawyers Committee's presentation to the disarmament discussions of today, given that the self-defense mission now functions as a core principle for many disarmament advocates.

Article 2(4) as a Prohibition or Limitation on the Use of Force? In a 1966 legal memorandum titled "The Legality of United States Participation in the Defense of Vietnam," the State Department argued that U.N. Charter article 2(4) "imposed an important limitation on the use of force by United Nations Members."[35] The Lawyers Committee, in response, argued that article 2(4) is not merely a "limitation" on force, but the "keystone to modern international law," and, as such, "outlaws" the threat and use of force as an instrument of foreign policy.[36]

Most scholars of international law recognize article 2(4) not as a "limitation" but as a "prohibition" on force. To cite one example, a former President of the International Court of Justice, Eduardo Jiménez de Arechaga, argued that "the paramount commitment of the [U.N.] Charter is Article 2, paragraph 4, which prohibits the threat or use of force in international relations. This is the cardinal rule of international law and the cornerstone of peaceful relations among states."[37] Note that Jiménez describes article 2(4) as a "prohibition" on force, the "paramount commitment of the Charter," and "the cardinal rule of international law." In contrast, the State Department's analysis of article 2(4), which established a precedent for the justification of a succession of military interventions from Vietnam to Panama (1989), demonstrates that the "limitation" interpretation permits the use of force in a wide range of scenarios, a development that hardly reflects the intent of this cardinal rule with regard to either limiting or prohibiting force.

Force as an Instrument of the World Community or the Nation-State? The Lawyers Committee acknowledged that the U.N. Charter stipulates that "for the very purpose of maintaining peace, various measures, and ultimately force may be required."[38] However, the charter authorizes the world community, acting through the Security Council, to decide what measures shall be taken with regard to the use of force.

According to the Lawyers Committee, "the essential meaning of this rule of international law [U.N.Charter article 39] is that no country shall decide for itself whether to use force, and, especially, whether to wage war through an intervention in a foreign conflict."[39] The World Court in *Nicaragua v. United States* (1986) ruled similarly in rejecting U.S. claims that its attacks against Nicaragua were justified through collective defense with El Salvador, stating that "there is no rule in customary international law permitting another State to exercise the right of collective self-defense on the basis of its own assessment of the situation."[40]

Article 51 as the Single, Narrow Exception to 2(4), or as Superseding 2(4)? The State Department argued that article 51 is a "saving clause" designed "to make clear that no other provision in the charter [specifically, article 2(4)] shall be interpreted to impair the inherent right of self-defense."[41] The Lawyers Committee responded as follows:

> The right of self-defense under the Charter arises only if an "armed attack" has occurred. The language of Article 51 is unequivocal on this point. The term "armed attack" has an established meaning in international law. It was deliberately employed in the Charter to reduce drastically the discretion of states to determine for themselves the scope of permissible self-defense both with regard to claims of individual and collective self-defense.[42]

Thus, as the Lawyers Committee argued, the resort to force in self-defense may be employed "only in the event that the victim state experiences an 'armed attack,' that is, if military forces cross an international boundary in visible, massive, and sustained form,"[43] and only where, in the words of Daniel Webster, "the necessity for action [is] instant, overwhelming, and leaving no choice of means, and no moment of deliberation."[44] Webster's description of the permissible basis for self-defense was adopted by the Nuremberg Tribunal in the case against major German war criminals.[45] Contrary, then, to what the State Department claimed, the Lawyers Committee argued that

> Article 51 purposely restricted the right of self-defense to a situation of armed attack because only these situations require immediate military reaction to avoid disaster. The rationale is persuasive: Other forms of aggression, especially indirect aggression, are so difficult to define and to ascertain, that too many situations might occur in which states, in good faith or bad, would claim the right of self-defense and thereby expand and intensify warfare.[46]

Collective Self-Defense as a Right of a State Under Armed Attack, or as the Inherent Right of an Intervening State? In the State Department's legal memorandum, the United States justified its military escalation in Vietnam by citing its "inherent" right to assist in the collective self-defense of South Vietnam in response to alleged North Vietnamese aggression.[47] In response, the Lawyers Committee argued that, as the U.S. military escalation in Vietnam demonstrated, a claim to an "inherent" right to intervene in foreign conflicts "may lead to the destruction of the assisted party, as well as to the widening of the local conflicts," and that "[i]t is to prevent such developments that Judge Jessup argues against interference by outside powers in such situations."[48] Philip C. Jessup, former judge on the World Court, wrote:

> It would be disastrous to agree that every State may decide for itself which of the two contestants is in the right and may govern its conduct according to its own decision. The ensuing conflict . . . would be disruptive to the ordered world community which the Charter and any modern law of nations must seek to preserve.[49]

Although the State Department's legal memorandum claimed that "Article 51 restates and preserves . . . a long-recognized . . . inherent right of self-defense,"[50] the Lawyers Committee observed that the memorandum "fails to cite any rule of general international law, or to establish any precedent to validate the 'inherent' right of outside states to participate in foreign conflicts."[51] In addition, the Lawyers Committee observed that "collective self-defense" is not found in writings on international law before the United Nations era, a fact difficult to reconcile with the claim that collective self-defense is an "inherent" right of an intervening state.[52]

The Lawyers Committee also cited the argument of Hans Kelsen, who wrote in 1950 that "[i]t is hardly possible to consider the right or duty of a non-attacked State to assist an attacked State as an 'inherent' right, that is to say, a right established by natural law."[53] Likewise, Julius Stone argued that "[u]nder general international law, a State has no right of 'self-defense' in respect to an armed attack on a third State."[54]

Rather than recognize an inherent right to third-party intervention under article 51, as the State Department suggested, the Lawyers Committee argued that the "inherent" right of collective self-defense resides primarily with the victim state, and that it is the responsibility of the world community, acting through the Security Council, to ensure the fulfillment of a victim state's right to collective self-defense once such a defense is formally requested by a victim state.

Relevance of the Vietnam Analysis

In calling into question the legality of U.S. intervention in Vietnam, the Lawyers Committee presented a general argument applicable to all such interventions, whether by the United States or any other state—hence, the relevance of the Lawyers Committee analysis to a discussion of disarmament and common security.

If it is the case that the cardinal rule of international law prohibits the use of force as an instrument of national policy; if it is the case that force is the rightful instrument of the world community under international law, and not a permissible policy instrument of an individual state; and if it is the case that the single, narrow exception to these two international law principles is the right of a state to use force to defend its territorial borders in response to an armed attack, then it would be difficult to imagine a credible disarmament and common security regime that did not incorporate these fundamental international law principles into an agreement on (a) standards of international conduct, and (b) a configuration of prohibited and permissible armaments.

Once international law principles are integrated into the disarmament and common security framework, the restrictions and ceilings placed upon military forces would be linked to legal prohibitions and legal rights that have been formally ratified by the international community, and that would apply across the board to all states. Therefore, since no state under international law possesses the right to use military force as an instrument of its national policy, under the terms of the Raskin Treaty each state's offense-capable conventional forces would be eliminated (according to the specifications of the World Security Agreement). At the same time, since each state possesses the international law right to defend itself in response to an armed attack upon its territorial borders, each state under the Raskin Treaty would be permitted to retain nonoffensive defense forces—that is, military forces sufficient only for the defense of its territorial borders (in accordance with the specifications of the World Security Agreement). And, since each state also possesses the right to collective self-defense in the event that it is the victim of armed attack, a U.N.-commanded collective defense and peacekeeping force would be maintained to fulfill a victim state's right to collective defense and to satisfy the peacekeeping obligations of the United Nations as outlined in chapter VII of the U.N. Charter.

Nonoffensive Defense and U.S. Presidential Powers

Elimination of the U.S. nuclear weapons arsenal and its offense-capable conventional forces as part of a global disarmament regime would not undermine the constitutional role of the U.S. president as commander-in-chief of the U.S. armed forces. In fact, the president's constitutional authority to deploy U.S. military forces, absent congressional authorization, does not exceed the self-defense mission. Once again the Vietnam example is illustrative.

In its 1966 memorandum on "The Legality of United States Participation in the Defense of Vietnam," the U.S. State Department asserted that President Johnson's authority as the chief executive of the United States and commander-in-chief of U.S. armed forces "carr[ied] very broad powers, including the power to deploy American forces abroad and commit them to military operations when the President deems such action necessary to maintain the security and defense of the United States."[55] Supporting this assertion on constitutional grounds, the State Department argued that

> [a]t the Federal Constitutional Convention in 1787, it was originally proposed that Congress have the power "to make war." There were objections that legislative proceedings were too slow for this power to be vested in Congress; it was suggested that the Senate might be a better repository. [James] Madison and [Elbridge] Gerry then moved to substitute "to declare war" for "to make war," "leaving to the Executive the power to repel sudden attacks." It was objected that this might make it too easy for the executive to involve the nation in war, but the motion carried with but one dissenting vote. In 1787, the world was a far larger place, and the framers probably had in mind attacks upon the United States. In the twentieth century, the world has grown much smaller. An attack on a country far from our shores can impinge directly on the nation's security.[56]

Responding to the State Department's reasoning, the Lawyers Committee on Vietnam observed that "the State Department's arguments militate against its own conclusions."[57] In other words, one cannot argue, as the State Department did in this instance, that since the constitutional framers confined the power of the president to deploy troops only in the defense of territorial borders, the president is therefore justified in sending U.S. troops abroad and committing them to military operations without authorization from the Congress and for reasons having nothing to do with the defense of U.S. borders. The "smaller world" scenario that was advanced by the State Department as justification for the Vietnam deployment provides no countervailing constitutional power to the president. The Lawyers Committee elaborated:

> Above all, the Founding Fathers restricted the power of the Executive to "repel sudden attacks." This expresses and foreshadows the philosophy of the United Nations Charter provisions and affirms what is being urged here: namely, that just as the framers of the Constitution accepted the need for special, carefully restricted powers "to repel sudden attacks," so did the framers of the United Nations Charter acknowledge the need of Member states for special, carefully restricted powers "if an armed attack occurs." Hence, for such emergencies, the United States Constitution permits an exception to the general rule that only Congress can declare war; and the Charter permits an exception from its general rule that only the Security Council can authorize military actions if international peace is threatened. From the standpoint of both instruments, the Constitution and the Charter, exceptional emergency measures are permitted to prevent disaster.[58]

The fact that the president possesses no constitutional authority to deploy the armed forces of the United States without prior congressional authorization, except for purposes relating to the immediate defense of U.S. borders, is well established by the constitutional text and the discernible intent of the framers. Regarding the president's war powers as prescribed by the Constitution, Michael Glennon, law professor at the University of California at Davis, writes: "It is clear that the Constitution's textual grants of war-making power to the President are paltry in comparison with, and are subordinate to, its grants to Congress."[59] According to the war powers authority as indicated in the constitutional text, only the Congress is authorized "to declare war," while the president, as "Commander in Chief," possesses the authority to conduct war once it is declared by Congress.[60] Referring to the constitutional limitations placed upon the president's war powers, James Madison, the principal author of the Constitution, wrote: "Those who are to conduct war cannot in the nature of things be the proper judges whether a war ought to be commenced, continued, or concluded."[61]

Regarding the president's war powers as indicated in the writings of the constitutional framers, Glennon writes: "There is no evidence that the Framers intended to confer upon the President any independent authority to commit the armed forces to combat, except in order to repel 'sudden attacks.'"[62] Indeed, referring again to the president's war powers, Madison wrote: "The Constitution supposes what the History of all Gov[ernments] demonstrates, that the Ex[ecutive] is the branch of power most interested in war & most prone to it. It has accordingly, with studied care, vested the question of war with the Legis[lature]."[63] Thomas Jefferson, while writing to Madison regarding the Constitution's war powers, stated: "We have already given in example one effectual check to the dog of war by transferring the power of letting him loose from the Executive to the Legislative body, from those who are to spend [the Executive] to those who are to pay [the Legislature]."[64]

Thus, a disarmament treaty that eliminated the offensive capabilities of the U.S. armed forces would not interfere with the president's constitutional authority as commander-in-chief, since the president possesses no constitutional authority to deploy offensive forces abroad without congressional authorization.[65] In fact, the president's discretionary authority to deploy U.S. troops is limited by the Constitution to those occasions that require an immediate military response in order to defend U.S. borders. And, as the Lawyers Committee pointed out, this constitutional limitation on the power of the commander-in-chief corresponds to U.N. Charter provisions relating to the use of force and self-defense.

The Raskin Treaty in Context

This final section will examine the Raskin Treaty within the context of other disarmament plans that have been issued recently by (a) the Center for Defense Information (CDI) in Washington, D.C.; (b) William Kaufmann and John Steinbruner at the Brookings Institution, also in Washington; and (c) Randall Forsberg at the Institute for Defense and Disarmament Studies in Boston.[66]

The Raskin proposal and each of these plans are quite different from the March 1992 Five-Year Defense Plan (FYDP) of the Bush administration,[67] and from a FYDP likely to be issued by President Clinton. The Bush administration had proposed military expenditures of $1.42 trillion from 1994 to 1999, whereas the Clinton presidential campaign had proposed spending $1.36 trillion over the same period. These high levels of military expenditures in both instances would pay for ongoing strategic nuclear weapons modernization as well as for regional and global intervention forces,[68] which, as stated in the Bush FYDP, will help guarantee "America's political and military mission in the post–cold war era . . . to insure that no rival superpower is allowed to emerge in Western Europe, Asia, or the territory of the Soviet Union."[69]

The disarmament and alternative security proposals from Raskin, Forsberg, CDI, and Brookings differ from the Bush and Clinton plans in three fundamental areas: Each of the disarmament plans proposes to change the mission of the U.S. armed forces from its current superpower mission to a primarily self-defense mission; each asserts the advantages of a cooperative security regime; and each would result in significantly reduced levels of military expenditures by the end of the decade. If the currently proposed FYDP was replaced by one of these alternative security plans, projected U.S. military expenditures could be reduced as follows: By the year 2000, Brookings projects a "cooperative security option" expenditure of $158 billion per year if its plan is adopted; CDI projects annual military expenditures of $104 billion if its proposal is adopted; and Forsberg estimates that annual U.S. military expenditures could be reduced to $70 billion by the year 2000 following implementation of her "common security policy," which in its broad outline is most similar to Raskin's proposal.[70] (By contrast, average projected U.S. military expenditures from 1994 to 1999 as proposed by both Bush and Clinton would be $270–$280 billion per year by the year 2000.)

Although the broad conceptual framework of each of the disarmament plans is similar, the international law foundation of Raskin's proposal is explicit and fundamental (see chapter I of the Raskin Treaty), whereas the correspondence to international law is marginal in the security models of Forsberg, CDI, and Brookings. The result is that, with regard to both the political and military standing of each state, the Raskin program is more precise, consistent, and equitable. For the purposes of a cooperative security regime that must take into account the legal obligations and legitimate rights of all states under international law, the presence or absence of these characteristics will most likely determine the success or failure of such a regime.

In the sections that remain, the common ground of cooperative security and self-defense that exists among the disarmament proposals is reviewed briefly, as are the differences in the specific formulation of these concepts.

Concepts in Common: Self-Defense and Cooperative Security

In a recent book titled *Decisions for Defense: Prospects for a New Order,* William Kaufmann and John Steinbruner formulate a "Cooperative Security Option" for U.S. policy planners to consider.[71] Under section heading "Basic Designs," Kaufmann and Steinbruner present their notion of a defense-oriented cooperative security regime:

> The underlying premise of a cooperative security arrangement is that the participating military organizations are all on the same side, are all defensively configured, and are all primarily committed to providing mutual reassurance. This requires them to simultaneously limit offensive capabilities that might support ground invasions or might undertake long-range bombardment to achieve some political objective. . . . If the

assumptions of cooperative security were actually adopted and the necessary regulations systematically implemented by the major military establishments—the United States, [the former] USSR, United Kingdom, France, Germany, Japan, and China, for example—they could legitimately be extended as a global security standard. It could be made very difficult in practical terms for any country to flout them. The reductions in the major powers' force levels and the restrictions on their offensive capability would be an undeniable benefit to all other military forces. Compliance with the rules could justifiably be demanded as a price for that benefit.... Moreover, with an internationally legitimized, highly inclusive security arrangement in place, compliance could readily be made a condition for access to international financial markets. That would be a much stronger incentive than any yet attempted.[72]

The authors suggest several technical refinements that would contribute to the practical feasibility of a defense-configured cooperative security program, including their description of "a common standard of density" requirement that would be applied to the ground forces of each participating nation:

> To inhibit the ability to assemble superior concentration of ground forces along a potential axis of attack, a standard ground force unit would be defined in terms of manpower and equipment, and ceilings would be set on the number of such units each military establishment could have. The number of units allowed would be normalized in terms of the extent of national territory to be defended so that countries follow a common standard of density (amount of force for a given amount of ground area) low enough to signal defensive rather than offensive intent.[73]

Kaufmann and Steinbruner state further that "[c]ontrolled concentration and movement" of these ground forces would be necessary because even "a common density standard would not preclude localized offensive concentrations." "Management of tactical air assets" would also be necessary "[b]ecause even defensively configured ground force operations can be severely degraded by precise tactical air attack." Because "the success of such attacks is highly sensitive to initiation and surprise, the composition of tactical air deployments would be regulated to favor defense over deep interdiction." Additionally, "the routine management of military air traffic would be internationalized in sensitive areas." And to help safeguard against regime breakout, "rules of disclosure would be imposed on basic research activities, new weapons deployment plans, and major operational exercises," and "integrated controls would be imposed on weapons exports and directly related technology." This latter provision "would involve the common licensing of all weapons transfers" and "enforced end-user disclosure for all related technology trade and continuous monitoring designed to detect any patterns of diversion."[74]

A recent *Defense Monitor* from the Center for Defense Information also proposes a defense-oriented military option for the United States.[75] CDI asserts that such an option could be fully implemented by the year 2000, and, if implemented, would reduce projected annual U.S. military expenditures to $104 billion by that year.[76]

CDI gets to its defense-oriented option by eliminating most traditional missions from U.S. military strategy. Using as its sources the president's "National Security Strategy of the United States," the "Annual Report to the Congress" from the secretary of defense, and the "National Military Strategy" from the Joint Chiefs of Staff, CDI identifies the current military missions of the United States as follows:

> 1. Defend continental United States.
> 2. Defend all U.S. territories.
> 3. Evacuate U.S. citizens from foreign countries in emergencies.
> 4. Assist in the defense of allies and friendly nations unable to defend themselves.
> 5. Intervene with military force in Third World nations to: deter aggression; counter terrorism; reduce flow of illegal drugs; ensure access to foreign markets for energy, oil, and minerals; maintain regional balances of power; combat threats to democracies from aggression, coercion, insurgencies, subversion, terrorism, and illicit drug trafficking.[77]

CDI comments, "Thoughtful appraisal of these missions raises questions as to whether all of them are still relevant."[78] Indeed, CDI recommends eliminating intervention in the Third World as well as the defense of allies and friendly nations as military missions.[79]

What remains as legitimate U.S. military missions according to the CDI proposal is described as follows:

> Strong forces for the defense of the United States and its territories would be retained. Some capacity to engage in military operations distant from the U.S. would remain but the role of world policeman would be abandoned. The development of alternatives to unilateral U.S. military action to deal with various instabilities, including ensuring access to oil, should be a priority of U.S. foreign policy between now and the end of the century.
>
> With a $104 billion annual military budget the United States would be an economic superpower but could not continue to project military power into every region of the world. It would behave more like other countries which limit their military objectives to self-defense. We would still be spending far more on the military than any other country is spending today. The U.S. would have forces available to participate in international peacekeeping, although it would not dominate such efforts. It would engage in truly collaborative joint military operations as needed.[80]

CDI argues that by abandoning its role as global policeman, significantly reducing its military expenditures, and reorienting the military mission of its armed forces primarily to self-defense, the United States "can help and support more actively the growing peacekeeping capabilities of the United Nations, the World Court, and other international bodies."[81]

Randall Forsberg's concept of a collective security system grounded in nonoffensive defense is summarized in a summer 1992 article in the *Boston Review:*

> The ultimate goal of a cooperative approach to security should be to demilitarize the international system: that is, to eliminate war and fear of war from the forefront of concern in the day-to-day conduct of international affairs; to severely restrict the scale and duration of minor wars that may still occur; to eliminate all weapons of mass destruction; and to minimize the economic and human burden of preparing for war and keeping the peace. In such a world, national military forces would be limited to small, stable, strictly nonoffensive defenses: a coast guard, a light air-defense system, border guards. The United Nations would command peacekeeping forces of somewhat greater range and power, whose purpose would be to help keep the peace and to safeguard against the emergence of militaristic leaders, bent on rebuilding aggressive military forces or acquiring weapons of mass destruction.[82]

Forsberg writes that implementation of this cooperative security regime "[o]ver the coming years . . . would allow the United States to reduce the $300 billion annual military budget not by just 25 percent ($75 billion) as proposed by the Pentagon, or by 50 percent ($150 billion) as proposed by the mainstream Brookings Institution, but by as much as 80 percent—that is, a savings on the order of $240 billion a year."[83]

Concepts and Conduct

Although there is common ground among the Raskin, Forsberg, CDI, and Brookings proposals with regard to cooperative security and self-defense as global security concepts, the Raskin proposal is unique among the others in that it also seeks to establish an accord on international conduct, grounded in international law, as part of the overall disarmament framework. The significance of an accord on conduct becomes apparent once one begins to examine the implications of the absence of such an accord. For example, there is no clearly defined criteria, legal or otherwise, in the other proposals that define, within the context of a cooperative security framework, when the unilateral use of force by states in the conduct of their international relations would be permissible or prohibited.

In the *Boston Review* article cited above, for example, Forsberg seems to imply that U.S. intervention might still be possible even within the context of her cooperative security proposal. Forsberg writes that the United States might retain three aircraft carriers (of which one would always be quickly available in a crisis), plus one division of Marines, together with a Marine air wing and amphibious assault ships. In the past such forces have been associated with unilateral intervention missions; but they could also provide useful support in multilateral peacekeeping missions.[84]

And in an article coauthored by Jonathan Dean and published in the summer 1992 issue of *International Security,* Forsberg and Dean appear to concede to the United States and to the great powers in general a "selective" right to Third World intervention in the post–cold war world:

> If large, standing conventional forces are no longer needed for East-West defense and deterrence in the post–Cold War world, to what extent are such forces needed or appropriate for great power intervention in Third World conflicts? Regional conflicts are no longer linked to the possibility of worldwide conventional and nuclear conflict between the United States and the former Soviet Union. They are regional only in most cases, not directly linked to the vital interests of others, and outside parties, including the United States, can be selective about becoming involved.[85]

A similar qualifying feature is found in CDI's general program with regard to the post–cold war order. In a 1991 issue of *Defense Monitor* titled, "U.S. Military Agenda for 1992 and Beyond," CDI recommends that the United States retain "a conventional military force designed to defend the U.S. and its territories rather than the borders of strong and wealthy Western Europe, Japan, and Korea; [and] powerful sea, air, and ground forces able to quickly go overseas to protect U.S. citizens or intervene for other reasons if necessary as a last resort."[86] Kaufmann and Steinbruner, as part of their cooperative security proposal, recommend the retention of reduced but still-powerful U.S. intervention forces that "would be capable of coordinating an operation of the size that was undertaken in the Persian Gulf but would be much less likely to encounter the need to do so."[87]

Although Forsberg, CDI, and Brookings would support unilateral U.S. intervention only as a "last resort," it is nevertheless a fact that both the capability for intervention and a general right of U.S. intervention are retained within the framework of their respective cooperative security proposals. Thus, the ultimate frequency of intervention would be determined not by these individuals or organizations but by the policies of successive groups of U.S. leaders, who would presumably be as free in the future as U.S leaders have been in the past to justify the resort to military intervention in the Third World as an action of "last resort." Within the context of this scenario, international law would have no more authority within the United States than it possesses today. Since other nations might also wish to retain interventionist forces for use "as a last resort," with a consequent proliferation of injury to international law, the obvious result would be an erosion of the cooperative security system as well as the collapse of nonoffensive defense (per Forsberg) and self-defense (per CDI and Brookings) as criteria for a cooperative security regime.

The Raskin Treaty, on the other hand, recognizes the legitimacy and legality of the use of force as a last resort only when the measures required in chapter VI of the U.N. Charter for the "Pacific Settlement of Disputes" have been exhausted and only when it is subsequently authorized by the world community acting through the U.N. Security Council, except when the unilateral use of force is necessary as a last resort by an individual state in response to an armed attack upon its territorial borders. Signatories to the Raskin Treaty would reaffirm this fundamental rule of international law pertaining to the prohibition of the use of force, and would agree to the abolition of weapons and forces possessing the capability to violate this rule. Due then to Raskin's efforts to integrate international conduct and disarmament concepts into a general accord on common security, the "selective" use of unilateral force as "a last resort" would be prohibited, the capability for resorting to offensive military actions would be abolished to the extent possible, and the cooperative security regime would be far less likely to break down in the manner described above.

Another component of Forsberg's proposal that is potentially inconsistent with international law is her assertion that "[t]he transition to a stable, fully cooperative global security system will involve a whole series of interlocking steps and changes," including "the spread of democratic institutions to countries that do not yet have them."[88] Forsberg argues that

> [a]s a result of such changes, we can expect to see a substantial strengthening in the international arena of the same norm regarding violence that obtains within nations with democratic values: that is, the view that it is never just or legitimate to use violence or armed force for any end except to defend against its (illegitimate) use by others who have not yet accepted this standard.[89]

Because there is no evidence suggesting that democratic states are less prone to resort to illegitimate international violence than states that are not democracies, and given the long-standing history of "democratization" as justification for great power intervention in the Third World and the fact that no state possesses the right under international law to impose a system of government upon another state, Forsberg's assertions in this regard do not lend themselves to building the framework of a fully cooperative security system, which, by definition, must take into account the legal rights of all states.

Although each state party to the Raskin Treaty would be required to guarantee the fulfillment of the rights of its citizens as required by the human rights conventions listed in Raskin Treaty article 2(4), these rights can be fulfilled through the establishment of political and economic systems that reflect the social and cultural diversity of the international community—members of which might not seek to duplicate the institutions and values of capitalist democracies.

Another area of concern within Forsberg's proposal is her recommendation regarding the maintenance of international forces for the purposes of U.N.-sponsored military actions. Forsberg writes that "one possible implementation [of United Nations forces for international peacekeeping purposes] would be for the United States, Japan, Germany, France, and Russia each to keep forces half as large as the Desert Storm–equivalent," which "would create a situation in which there would be more than enough forces at the disposal of the UN Security Council to respond to an act of aggression anywhere in the world, but no capability for large-scale unilateral military intervention by any single nation."[90] Given that the Desert Storm deployment consisted of 500,000 well-equipped and highly lethal troops, the suggestion that each of the great powers maintain an interventionary force of 250,000 troops is inconsistent with the nonoffensive defense criterion of Forsberg's cooperative security system.

One should keep in mind that the United States deployed far fewer than 250,000 troops in each of its interventions against Nicaragua, Grenada, Libya, and Panama in the 1980s. Since these kinds of interventions were not "large-scale military intervention[s]" in the Desert Storm sense, one must assume, given the implications of those aspects of Forsberg's program discussed in this section, that these kinds of interventions would still be possible within the framework of her proposal. Therefore, the maintenance of great power intervention forces at one-half Desert Storm capability, and available perhaps for "selective" use as a "last resort" in a number of possible military theaters (which presumably would be demilitarized per Forsberg's program), would be inconsistent with a cooperative security model. The geopolitical product most likely to develop out of such an arrangement would not be an international order that respected the legal rights of all nations, but a global system of regional hegemons—the United States in the Western hemisphere, Japan in southeast Asia, China in central Asia, the Soviet Union within the Commonwealth of Independent States, and Germany and France in Europe.

Admittedly, the question regarding the maintenance of international forces available for use by the United Nations, as prescribed in article 43 of the U.N. Charter, presents formidable logistical problems to a cooperative security regime based upon the nonoffensive defense doctrine. However, the precise "numbers and types of forces, their degree of readiness and general location, and the nature of the facilities and assistance to be provided" to the United Nations (see U.N. Charter article 43[2]) would need to be negotiated in a manner consistent with the broad principles and goals of the cooperative security framework. Although the Raskin regime does not make specific recommendations in this regard, it does provide a negotiating framework that is consistent with the broad objectives of the cooperative security model (see Raskin Treaty article 2[6] and the corresponding article in the treaty commentary).

Finally, the Raskin Treaty regime would require the abolition of nuclear weapons, whereas CDI and Brookings propose that the United States maintain a minimum-deterrence strategic nuclear arsenal of 1,000 to 3,000 warheads.[91] If it is the case that within the framework of the CDI and Brookings proposals some states would maintain a right to possess and deploy nuclear weapons while other states would be denied that right, such a claim to exclusive rights regarding nuclear weapons would be fundamentally incompatible with a cooperative security regime grounded in international law for two reasons: (a) nuclear weapons, including possession, deployment, targeting, and threatened use, are illegal under international law; and (b) the denial to some states of legal privileges and exemptions granted to other states would be inherently subversive of the essential nature of a cooperative security regime. Under the terms of the Raskin Treaty, which is grounded in fundamental principles of international law, all states are juridically equal. Therefore, within the framework of Raskin's proposal, no state would be permitted to claim exemptions from legal obligations or special rights not available to other states, including with regard to nuclear weapons.

Conclusion

Although there is an emerging consensus regarding cooperative security and territorial defense as the basic constituents of a new global security framework, this framework needs to be integrated into the world order design of international law as expressed in its fundamental rules, principles, and procedures so that universal and nondiscriminatory standards of military policy and international conduct can be achieved.

Notes to Chapter 4

1. See the 1925 Geneva Protocol for the Prohibition of the Use in War of Asphyxiating, Poisonous or Other Gases, and of Bacteriological Methods of Warfare; the 1972 Convention on the Prohibition of Development, Production and Stockpiling of Bacteriological (Biological) and Toxin Weapons and on their Destruction; and the 1992 Convention on the Prohibition of the Development, Production, Stockpiling, and Use of Chemical Weapons and on their Destruction.

2. Elliott L. Meyrowitz, *Prohibition of Nuclear Weapons: The Relevance of International Law* (Dobbs Ferry: Transnational Publishers, Inc., 1990), 29-39; 222-229.

The official, declared position of the United States with regard to nuclear weapons and international law is found in its military manuals. The U.S. Navy's military manual for 1955 states (Meyrowitz, 29): "There is at present no rule of international law expressly prohibiting states from the use of nuclear weapons in warfare. In the absence of express prohibition, the use of such weapons against enemy combatants and other military objectives is permitted." The U.S. Army's military manual for 1956 states (Meyrowitz, 30): "The use of explosive 'atomic weapons,' whether by air, sea, or land forces, cannot as such be regarded as violative of international law in the absence of any customary rule of international law or international convention restricting their employment." Meyrowitz writes (31): "Despite the evolution of United States strategic doctrine since 1956, the official United States position on the legal status of nuclear weapons as found in its military manuals has remained unchanged, even with the official endorsement in Presidential Directive 59 of a limited nuclear war policy."

The British government's "formula for determining the legality of nuclear weapons" is expressed in the British Manual of Military Law (Meyrowitz, 224): "In the absence of any rule of international law dealing expressly with it, the use which may be made of a particular weapon will be governed by the ordinary rules and the question of the legality of its use in any particular case will, therefore, involve merely the application of the recognized principles of international law. "

The position of the Soviet government has been described in Peter B. Maggs, "The Soviet Viewpoint on Nuclear Weapons and International Law," 29 *Law & Contemporary Problems* 956, 957 (1964) (cited in Meyrowitz, 224):

> The official manual of naval law published in 1956 by the Soviet Ministry of Defense gives tacit approval to the legality of the use of nuclear weapons against military targets. In its discussion of forbidden weapons, it not only refrains from stating that the use of nuclear weapons is illegal, but specifically points out that no international convention banning their use in time of war exists. In contrast, aerial bombardment of cities with nuclear weapons is condemned specifically in a later section of the book. The textbook of international law published in 1964 and officially approved for use in Soviet law schools also refrains from any direct statement that the military use of nuclear weapons is illegal.

Meyrowitz writes (224): "The aforesaid position contrasts with the opinions of leading Soviet legal scholars. Authorities such as Bogdanov, Romashkin, Korovin, Trainin, and Dordenevski have all concluded that the use of nuclear weapons is illegal."

3. Meyrowitz, *Prohibition of Nuclear Weapons*, 30.

4. For information on the strategic nuclear war-fighting plan of the United States, see Peter Pringle and William Arkin, *S.I.O.P.: The Secret U.S. Plan for Nuclear War* (New York: W.W. Norton & Company, 1983); Michio Kaku and Daniel Axelrod, *To Win a Nuclear War: The Pentagon's Secret War Plans* (Boston: South End Press, 1987); Robert Scheer, *With Enough Shovels: Reagan, Bush and Nuclear War* (New York: Random House, 1983).

5. See "Statement on the Illegality of Nuclear Warfare of the Lawyers Committee on Nuclear Policy," in Francis A. Boyle, Alfred P. Rubin, Burns H. Weston, Sean MacBride, Richard A. Falk, Dorothy Hodgkin, Maurice Wilkins, and Peter Weiss, *In re: More Than 50,000 Nuclear Weapons: Analyses of the Illegality of Nuclear Weapons Under International Law* (Northampton: Aletheia Press, 1991), 107-111.

6. See, for example, Boyle, et al., *In re: More Than 50,000 Nuclear Weapons*.

7. C. G. Weeramantry, *Nuclear Weapons and Scientific Responsibility* (Wolfeboro: Longwood Academic, 1987), 83-84.

8. The London Nuclear Warfare Tribunal, *The Bomb and the Law* (Stockholm: The Alva and Gunnar Myrdal Foundation, 1989); excerpts reprinted in Boyle, et al., *In re: More Than 50,000 Nuclear Weapons*, 93.

9. See U.N.G.A. Res. 1653 (XVI).

10. See U.N.G.A. Res. 33/71 B; U.N.G.A. Res. 35/152 D; U.N.G.A. Res. 36/92 I; U.N.G.A. Res. 45/59 A; and U.N.G.A. Res. 46/37 D.

11. See Leland M. Goodrich and Edvard Hambro, *Charter of the United Nations: Commentary and Documents* (Boston: World Peace Foundation, 1949), 150-168.

12. See Nicholas Grief, *The World Court Project on Nuclear Weapons and International Law* (Northampton: Aletheia Press, 1992).

13. See Boyle, et al., *In re: More Than 50,000 Nuclear Weapons*, 24.

14. *Ibid.*, 69-70.

15. *Ibid.*, 24.

16. *Ibid.*, 111.

17. Grief, *The World Court Project*, 15.

18. Boyle, et al., *In re: More Than 50,000 Nuclear Weapons*, 94.

19. *Ibid.*, 94-95.

20. *Ibid.*, 97.

21. *Ibid.*, 95.

22. *Ibid.*, 95.

23. Weeramantry, *Nuclear Weapons and Scientific Responsibility*, 103-05.

24. Boyle, et al., *In re: More Than 50,000 Weapons*, 93.

25. See U.N. Charter article 2(4).

26. See Article VI, section (a) of the Nuremberg Principles, which defines "crimes against peace" as " (i) [p]lanning, preparation, initiation or waging of a war

of aggression or a war in violation of international treaties, agreements or assurances" and as "(ii) [p]articipation in a common plan or conspiracy for the accomplishment of any of the acts mentioned under (i)."

27. In a special issue on nonoffensive defense published in the September 1988 issue of *The Bulletin of the Atomic Scientists,* contributors described nonoffensive defense as follows.

The editor of the *Bulletin's* special issue on nonoffensive defense, Hal Harvey, director of the security program at the Rocky Mountain Institute in Colorado, wrote: "The idea is to rearrange conventional forces so that they can defend but not attack. Under such monikers as 'nonoffensive defense' (the main term used in these articles), 'nonprovocative defense,' 'defensive defense,' 'reasonable sufficiency,' and 'mutual defense superiority,' these proposals suggest that nations can restructure weapons, personnel, and strategy to assure their own military security without posing a threat to other nations." Harvey, "Defense Without Aggression," 12.

Paul Rogers, who chaired the U.K. Alternative Defense Commission from 1984 to 1987, wrote: "Nonoffensive defense has been applied almost entirely to Europe rather than to matters of global strategy. The latter application, however, is at least as important because offensive strategies pervade superpower planning and force postures in the strategic and global conventional arena." Rogers, "The Nuclear Connection," 20.

Andrei A. Kokoshin, deputy-director of the Institute on the U.S.A. and Canada in Moscow, wrote: "The idea of bringing defensive character into military doctrines and planning, making them develop strictly in this direction, is an important factor in providing reliable mutual security and in strengthening stability.... Convergence in the direction of strictly defensive force structures and strategies on both sides would create a synthesis of conditions which could reduce political and military tension in Europe and in the world as a whole, and could open the way to a nuclear-free world." Kokoshin, "Restructure Forces, Enhance Security," 37.

Randall Forsberg, director of the Institute for Defense and Disarmament Studies in Boston, Massachusetts, wrote: "The concept of nonoffensive defense is central to developing a truly stable and enduring international peace, characterized by a demilitarized, democratic international system; the lowest safe levels of standing armed forces and military spending; and greatly reduced nuclear arsenals—in general, conditions that ultimately will make thinkable the complete abolition of nuclear weapons. For these reasons, nonoffensive defense should be the ultimate goal of arms limitation and reduction." Forsberg, "Toward a Nonaggressive World," 49.

28. See, in regard to Afghanistan, *The New York Times,* Dec. 31, 1979 and Jan. 4, 1980; in regard to Czechoslovakia, *The New York Times,* Aug. 21–24, 1968; and in regard to Hungary, *The New York Times,* Nov. 3–7, 1956.

29. In a legal memorandum issued on March 4, 1966, the U.S. State Department asserted that "[t]he United States and South Vietnam Have the Right under International Law to Participate in the Collective Defense of South Vietnam against Armed Attack." See "The Legality of United States Participation in the Defense of Vietnam," Memorandum from the Department of State, Office of the Legal Adviser, March 4, 1966, reprinted in The Lawyers Committee on American Policy Towards

Vietnam, Richard Falk, Chair, John H.E. Fried, Rapporteur, *Vietnam and International Law: An Analysis of International Law and the Use of Force, and the Precedent of Vietnam for Subsequent Interventions,* (Northampton: Aletheia Press, 1990), 135.

On October 26, 1983, the day after the U.S. invasion of Grenada, the U.S. State Department issued a two-page memorandum which cited "collective defense" with the nations of the Organization of Eastern Caribbean States as the legal basis for invading Grenada.

On April 14, the day of the U.S. bombing of Libya, President Ronald Reagan, in a nationally televised broadcast, stated that the bombing was "fully consistent with Article 51 of the United Nations Charter."

On December 20, 1989, the day of the U.S. invasion of Panama, U.S. Secretary of State James Baker stated that the invasion was justified "in accordance with international law" as follows: "The United States, under international law, has an inherent right of self-defense as recognized in Article 51 of the United Nations Charter and Article 21 of the Organization of American States Charter, which entitles us to take measures necessary to defend our military personnel, our United States nationals, and U.S. installations."

In response to Nicaragua's legal challenge at the International Court of Justice to U.S. military and paramilitary actions in and against Nicaragua, the United States responded outside of the context of the subsequent proceedings at the ICJ by asserting that U.S. military and paramilitary attacks in and against Nicaragua were carried out in the collective defense of El Salvador and were therefore justified under international law.

30. Addressing the United Nations on December 7, 1988, then Soviet President Mikhail Gorbachev stated that "the use or threat of force no longer can or must be an instrument of foreign policy," that the prohibition against force "is the first and the most important component of a nonviolent world," and that "states must to some extent review their attitude toward the United Nations." *The New York Times,* December 8, 1988. Referring to Gorbachev's remarks in its editorial the next day, *The New York Times* commented that "[i]t's disingenuous for him to say that 'the use or threat of force no longer can or must be an instrument of foreign policy.'" *The New York Times,* December 9, 1988.

31. The response of *The New York Times* to Gorbachev's December 7 address to the United Nations was representative of the overall response of the political establishment in the United States to Gorbachev's disarmament efforts. From March 1985 to December 1987, the United States rejected nearly a dozen Soviet offers to join in halting nuclear weapons tests; conducted 26 nuclear tests during the eighteen-month period when the Soviets had unilaterally stopped testing nuclear weapons; rejected pleas on at least four occasions from other nations to join the Soviets in a nuclear test ban; rejected Soviet proposals to freeze deployment of new strategic nuclear weapons while arms-control talks in Geneva were under way; repudiated the 1979 SALT II Treaty by exceeding that treaty's numerical ceiling on ballistic missiles; rejected a Soviet proposal for a forty-nation conference to establish an international organization that would monitor a ban on space weapons; conducted

provocative anti-satellite (ASAT) weapons tests despite Soviet proposals to ban both sides from testing ASATs; abstained on a U.N. General Assembly resolution calling on the United States and Soviet Union to produce an arms control agreement that would end the nuclear arms race; and boycotted a U.N. Conference on Disarmament and Development that proposed establishing an international fund for Third World development with money saved from arms control and disarmament agreements.

32. *The MacNeil-Lehrer News Hour,* November 19, 1992.

33. Signatories to the Lawyers Committee's rebuttal to the State Department's legal memorandum were Richard A. Falk, (Chair), John H.E. Fried, Richard J. Barnet, John H. Herz, Stanley Hoffmann, Wallace McClure, Saul H. Mendlovitz, Richard S. Miller, Hans J. Morgenthau, William G. Rice, Burns H. Weston, and Quincy Wright.

34. The Lawyers Committee on Vietnam, *Vietnam and International Law,* 14.

35. "The Legality of United States Participation in the Defense of Vietnam," Memorandum from the Department of State, Office of the Legal Adviser, March 4, 1966, reprinted in The Lawyers Committee on Vietnam, *Vietnam and International Law,* 137.

36. The Lawyers Committee on Vietnam, *Vietnam and International Law,* 20.

37. See *Case Concerning Military and Paramilitary Activities in and Against Nicaragua (Nicaragua v. United States of America) (Merits),* 1986, ICJ Rep. 14 (Judgment of June 27, 1986).

38. The Lawyers Committee on Vietnam, *Vietnam and International Law,* 20.

39. *Ibid.,* 20.

40. See remarks of Carlos Arguello Gomez in *Nicaragua v. United States,* 1984.

41. State Department memorandum, reprinted in The Lawyers Committee on Vietnam, *Vietnam and International Law,* 137-38.

42. The Lawyers Committee on Vietnam, *Vietnam and International Law,* 21-22.

43. *Ibid.,* 22.

44. *Ibid.,* 22.

45. *Ibid.,* 22.

46. *Ibid.,* 24.

47. State Department memorandum, reprinted in The Lawyers Committee on Vietnam, *Vietnam and International Law,* 135-38.

48. The Lawyers Committee on Vietnam, *Vietnam and International Law,* 28, 25.

49. *Ibid.,* 25.

50. State Department memorandum, reprinted in The Lawyers Committee on Vietnam, *Vietnam and International Law,* 137-38.

51. The Lawyers Committee on Vietnam, *Vietnam and International Law,* 28.

52. *Ibid.,* 28-30.

53. *Ibid.,* 27.

54. *Ibid.,* 28.

55. State Department memorandum, reprinted in The Lawyers Committee on Vietnam, *Vietnam and International Law,* 149.

56. *Ibid.,* 149.

57. The Lawyers Committee on Vietnam, *Vietnam and International Law,* 95.

58. *Ibid.*, 95.
59. Michael Glennon, *Constitutional Diplomacy* (Princeton: Princeton University Press, 1990), 72.
60. See Glennon, *Constitutional Diplomacy,* 72-74.
61. *Ibid.*, 83.
62. *Ibid.*, 81.
63. *Ibid.*, 82-83.
64. *Ibid.*, 83.
65. In *Dellums v. Bush,* fifty-four members of Congress sought to prevent President Bush from initiating offensive military action against Iraq without securing a declaration of war or other explicit congressional authorization for such action. In his opinion on the central political question involved in the case, Judge Harold H. Greene, United States District Court, District of Columbia, wrote the following: "It is appropriate first to sketch out briefly the constitutional and legal framework in which the current controversy arises. Article I, Section 8, Clause 11 of the Constitution grants to the Congress the power 'To declare War.' To the extent that this unambiguous direction requires construction, it is provided by the framers' comments that they felt it to be unwise to entrust the momentous power to involve the nation in a war to the President alone; Jefferson explained that he desired 'an effectual check to the Dog of war'; James Wilson similarly expressed the expectation that this system would guard against hostilities being initiated by a single man." In a footnote to his opinion, Judge Greene also wrote: "While the Constitution itself speaks only of the congressional power to declare war, it is silent on the issue of the effect of a congressional vote that war not be initiated. However, if the War Clause is to have its normal meaning, it excludes from the power to declare war all branches other than the Congress. It also follows that if the Congress decides that the United States forces should not be employed in foreign hostilities, and if the Executive does not of its own volition abandon participation in such hostilities, action by the courts would appear to be the only available means to break the deadlock in favor of the constitutional provision." *Dellums v. Bush,* 752 F. Supp. 1141, 1144 (D.D.C. 1990).
66. See the Center for Defense Information (CDI), "Defending America: CDI Options for Military Spending," *The Defense Monitor,* vol. XXI. no. 4, 1992; "U.S. Military Agenda for 1992 and Beyond," *The Defense Monitor,* vol. XX, no. 6, 1991; and "What Should We Defend?: A New Military Strategy for the United States," *The Defense Monitor,* vol. XVII, no. 4, 1988; William W. Kaufmann and John D. Steinbruner, *Decisions for Defense: Prospects for a New Order* (Washington, D.C.: The Brookings Institution, 1991); Jonathan Dean and Randall Watson Forsberg, "CFE and Beyond: The Future of Conventional Arms Control," *International Security,* vol. 17, no. 1, Summer 1992; Randall Forsberg, "Defense Cuts and Cooperative Security in the Post–Cold War World," Institute for Defense and Disarmament Studies, 1992, reprinted with permission from the *Boston Review,* vol. XVII, nos. 3-4, May-July 1992; Randall Forsberg, "US Needs Policy of Common Security and Military Cuts of 80%," *Peacework,* no. 217, March 1992; Randall Watson Forsberg, "UN Peacemaking in the post–Cold War World," Institute for Defense and Disarmament Studies, April 1992; and Institute for Defense and Disarmament Studies,

"Developing a Cooperative Security Regime: A Case Study of Potential International Cooperation in Restricting the Deployment, Production, and Export of Supersonic Fighter-Attack Aircraft," March 1992.

67. See CDI, "Defending America," 1.

68. See Forsberg, "Defense Cuts and Cooperative Security," for a summary of Congressman Les Aspin's approach to long-term military strategy, production, and spending. Aspin was Governor Bill Clinton's military advisor during the 1992 presidential campaign. He has been appointed by President-elect Clinton to serve as secretary of defense. It is likely that Aspin's plan will serve as the basis for President Clinton's five-year defense plan.

69. *The New York Times,* March 8, 1992.

70. Kaufmann and Steinbruner, *Decisions for Defense,* 74; CDI, "Defending America," 1, 5; Forsberg, "Defense Cuts and Cooperative Security," 9.

71. See Kaufmann and Steinbruner, *Decisions for Defense,* 67-76.

72. *Ibid.,* 70, 71-72.

73. *Ibid.,* 70.

74. *Ibid.,* 70, 71.

75. See CDI, "Defending America."

76. *Ibid.,* 5.

77. *Ibid.,* 4.

78. *Ibid.,* 4.

79. *Ibid.,* 4, 5.

80. *Ibid.,* 5.

81. *Ibid.,* 7.

82. Forsberg, "Defense Cuts and Cooperative Security," 7.

83. Forsberg, "US Needs Policy of Common Security and Military Cuts of 80%," 1.

84. Forsberg, "Defense Cuts and Cooperative Security," 9.

85. Dean and Forsberg, "CFE and Beyond," 107.

86. CDI, "U.S. Military Agenda for 1992 and Beyond," 7.

87. Kaufmann and Steinbruner, *Decisions for Defense,* 74.

88. Forsberg, "Defense Cuts and Cooperative Security," 7.

89. *Ibid.,* 7.

90. Forsberg, "Defense Cuts and Cooperative Security," 9.

91. See CDI, "Defending America," 6; Kaufmann and Steinbruner, *Decisions for Defense,* 73, 75. Forsberg advocates the maintenance of "'minimum deterrent' forces, to be maintained for a transitional period until a cooperative security system encompassing all nations is firmly entrenched and working smoothly." Forsberg, "Defense Cuts and Cooperative Security," 9.